BILLY GRAHAM—No man or woman is too high or too low, too old or too young, to come under his spiritual spell!

Billy Graham has affected the Christian world as no man has in the past 50 years. Today, he has over 30 million followers.

In this highly readable, inspiring biography, you will meet Billy Graham—the boy and the man—and read what he thinks about life and God and everyday living.

Everyone interested in Billy Graham—the man or his message to the world—will want to read this rewarding book.

BILLY GRAHAM

The Man Who Walks With God

Glenn Daniels

PAPERBACK LIBRARY, Inc.
New York

PAPERBACK LIBRARY EDITION

First Printing: *June, 1961*
Second Printing: *October, 1964*
Third Printing: *June, 1967*

Copyright, 1961, by Glenn Daniels

All rights reserved. This book, or parts thereof, may not be reproduced without permission.

Paperback Library books are published by Paperback Library, Inc. Its trademark, consisting of the words "Paperbeck Library" and associated distinctive design, is registered in the United States Patent Office. Printed in the United States of America, Paperback Library, Inc., 260 Park Avenue South, New York, N.Y. 10010.

*TO ALL THOSE
WHO HAVE HEARD BILLY GRAHAM
... AND BELIEVED*

Chapter I

The big alarm clock went off at three o'clock in the morning. Its shrill clatter pierced the sleep of the boy in the bed and he stirred. From habit he reached out for the clock, but the morning was cold: he shivered and buried his arm under the covers again. After a minute, the alarm slowed, then stopped. Half-awake now, the boy let himself enjoy the warmth of his bed and the silence of the room. He could hear sounds from his parents' room, down the hall. The muffled voices of his mother and father reminded him that he ought to get up; there was work to be done. But he could not bring himself to move. Relaxing, he let sleep settle upon him.

There was a soft tap on his door. "Billy Frank?"

"Yes, Ma?"

"Don't fall asleep."

"No, Ma."

He listened to his mother's footsteps as they moved from his door to the top of the stairs, then down them and into the kitchen. A car pulled up. The slam of its door seemed unusually loud in the early morning. Then there were steps on the back porch and the kitchen door was opened and closed. Billy heard:

"Morning, Mrs. Graham."

"Morning, Charlie."

"Feels like it's gonna be a cold day."

"It does, doesn't it? I'll have some hot coffee for you in a minute."

"Fine. Are the boys up?"

1

"Melvin is, I think, but Billy Frank seems to be having a hard time of it this morning."

The hired man laughed softly. "Too much baseball, I guess."

"I guess so."

Billy realized he could not much longer postpone the ordeal of getting up. He gave himself a minute more, during which he heard his brother Melvin go downstairs, then his father. They would, he knew, all be waiting for him in the kitchen, ready to start the day. With a deep sigh of resignation, Billy swept back the covers and swung himself to his feet. At 17, he was tall for his age, almost six feet. His body was lean and firm, his muscles hardened by his daily chores on his father's farm and hours spent at the baseball games he loved.

Familiar with every inch of his room, he did not need a light to dress. Quickly he slipped into the heavy jeans and the extra shirt and sweater he felt would be required on so cold a morning. Then he hurried downstairs to the warm kitchen.

"Good morning," he said as he entered.

The others returned his greeting.

He listened to their talk as he poured hot water into a pan in the sink and washed his hands and face. He could smell the fresh coffee as he drew a comb through his blonde wavy hair. Finished, he turned to the cup of coffee that awaited him and took a sip. He glanced at his father and saw that the man was awaiting his attention. Billy put down the cup and nodded.

The five people in the kitchen lowered their heads. Frank Graham said: "Dear Lord, we dedicate this day to you. Guide us through the day so that our thoughts and deeds will be to your glory. Amen."

The others added: "Amen."

Billy took another sip of coffee, then reached for one of the doughnuts his mother had made the day before and jammed it into his pocket. At the door he removed his cap from a peg and flipped it onto his head—casually but carefully, to protect the blonde waves that the fellows at school always teased him about but the girls openly admired. Then he followed his brother, his father and the hired man out the door and across to the barn.

The crisp air of the North Carolina morning chilled the last remnants of sleep from Billy's eyes. Even so, he made his way to the barn without actually watching his steps. And yet he did not have to watch his steps: he knew the path by heart.

He had been born on the farm on November 7, 1918. His father had been born there as well. It was his grandfather, born on a ship that brought his emigrant parents from Ulster, who had bought the farm before the Civil War and had started the dairy business by which the family still supported itself. Billy's father—William Franklin Graham, after whom he was named—had been born in a log cabin. By the time of his marriage, a two-story farm house stood on the farm, and into it he moved his new wife, Morrow Coffey, whose family had settled in North Carolina before the American Revolution. The four Graham children, of whom Billy was the oldest, were born in the frame house. When Billy was nine, his father built a new house, this one of brick, and the special feature of it that made it the talk of rural Mecklenburg County was its indoor plumbing. No longer did the Graham children have to bathe in a washtub on the back porch or walk to the foot of the hill to the Chick Sale.

When the new house was built, Billy Frank, as his family called him, could already consider himself a working man. His father had a farmer's practical attitude towards children: they should all have chores when they become old enough to assume responsibility. Billy was eight when his father began to awaken him each morning to help milk the dairy's 75 cows. At ten, he had the reputation of being one of the fastest milkers in the county. At twelve, he was taught to drive, and each morning after the milking he drove a truck through the dawn-streets of nearby Charlotte while a hired man trotted to backdoors to deliver the cream and milk. At fifteen, Billy had a route of his own.

Ordinarily, it would have been expected that Billy should follow his father into the dairy business, but this was not the case. Billy wanted to become a professional baseball player and his family did nothing to stand in his way. At the young age of fifteen, he was already a semi-professional first-baseman, receiving fifteen dollars a game when he was called upon to play, which was about four or five times each season. It was during this period of his life that the New York Yankees, returning from spring training, stopped at Charlotte for an exhibition game. In a gesture of good will, Babe Ruth visited the suburban diamond where Billy's team worked out. Before leaving, Ruth beckoned to Billy.

"I've been watching you at first base," Ruth said. "You're pretty good. Are you serious about baseball?"

"Yes, sir, I sure am," Billy said.

Babe Ruth studied Billy's lanking form. "Good. You've got the build for it. Keep at it, son, and maybe one of these days I'll be seeing you in Yankee Stadium."

Frank Graham secretly hoped otherwise. In his own youth, Frank Graham had wanted to become a minister. Only the demands of helping his father on the farm kept him from it. Later when the farm began to prosper, Frank considered himself too old to begin the long studies. But he never lost the ambition. When his first son was born, Frank Graham inwardly hoped that the boy would pursue the vocation that had been denied him. Certainly the atmosphere in the Graham household was conducive to that.

Frank Graham began each workday with a prayer, dedicating the day to God. The Bible was read at the breakfast table after the meal, and as the children grew old enough they were expected to learn a new Bible verse each day. In the evening, the Bible and other spiritual books were read by the family in the livingroom before going to bed. On Sundays, the family attended both the morning and evening services at the nearby Presbyterian church to which they belonged and in which all the children were baptized. During winters, a social event at the Graham house was confined to singing hymns with neighbors, with the evening brought to an end with cocoa and cake for all.

Frank Graham belonged to a group of businessmen who shared his interest in religion. Once a week they gathered in Charlotte for lunch and a talk by one of the local ministers. Once a month they spent a whole day together in prayer and meditation. One summer month when Billy was nine, the group gathered at the Graham farm for its day of retreat. To escape the noise of the house and the barns, the men went into the quiet orchard where they could conduct their spiritual exercises without distraction. It was the era of the Roaring Twenties, the frantic years when many Americans, giddy from rising prosperity and dizzy on bootleg whiskey, lived only for pleasure. As the nation's profits soared, however, the nation's morals sank. Frank Graham was aware of it, and he was distressed by it.

"What kind of world will our children inherit?" he asked his friends as their retreat-day came to an end. "There is only one hope for us. America needs a new spiritual leader, someone who loves the Lord above everything else and is willing to devote his life to converting others to Him."

"That's right, Frank," one of the men said, "but where can we find a man like that?"

Another man said: "Yes, that's the problem. We sure could use an evangelist like that, but where is he?"

It was at this moment that Billy Graham came home from an afternoon of baseball to do his evening chores. As he climbed the grassy hill from the road to the house, he glanced towards the orchards and saw the men there. He paused and watched them for a moment. Several of them seemed to be looking at him; he waved to them.

Frank Graham waved back. So did three or four of the other men. None of them realized that the person they were seeking was right there before their eyes.

ii

The barn was warm. Entering it, Billy shivered as he shook off the morning's cold. The cows heard the four workers come in and greeted them with brief bellows of impatience. Frank Graham clicked on the overhead lights, then went to prepare the pasteurizing and separating machines. Melvin occupied himself with the equipment that steamed the milk bottles. Billy and Charlie got their stools and buckets and began to milk the cows. Each man knew his job and worked at it steadily; there was little conversation. By five o'clock, the two trucks were loaded. Billy slipped behind the wheel of one; Charlie took the other. Each headed for different parts of Charlotte for the monotonous task of trotting from the truck to a threshold, depositing fresh milk and picking up empty bottles, then trotting back to the truck, driving a few feet and then repeating the process.

There were times, however, when Billy put the routine to good advantage. Starting in the spring and continuing throughout the summer, he looked upon his job as a kind of baseball practice. For him, the trotting back and forth provided an opportunity to build up his stamina. Some mornings he would actually run between the truck and the thresholds, just to see how long he could keep up the pace without tiring. And if the hour was early enough and the streets abandoned Billy was not behond sliding the last few feet to a threshold or to occupy himself on the way back to the truck by throwing the empty bottles high into the air to practice catching pop-flies. Any early riser who saw him at these antics would wonder if the milkman had suddenly gone out of his mind, but those who knew him appreciated his love of baseball and were amused.

Usually he was home shortly before seven. This gave him time to wash, change clothes for school and be at the breakfast table by seven-thirty. The men of the family had by now worked up enormous appetites from their morning's labor, but nevertheless the women had also been busy. The two daughters, Catherine and Jean, had been up since six, cleaning the house, feeding the chickens and pigs, and, in the summer, picking the day's fresh vegetables. In the autumn they helped with the canning, and once a month they gathered at the kitchen table with Frank and Morrow Graham to prepare the bills for the dairy's 400 customers. Breakfast, then, was a big meal, with hot cereal, eggs, meat, grits, mountains of toast and pitchers of fresh milk.

The meal finished, Frank Graham reached for his Bible. "All right, Billy Frank," he said, "we'll start with you this morning. How far are you with the Ninetieth Psalm?"

"The fifteenth verse," Billy said.

"You learned it yesterday?"

"Yes, Dad."

"Then let's hear it."

Billy closed his eyes in an effort to see the words in his mind, then he recited: "Make us glad according to the days wherein thou has afflicted us and the years wherein we have done evil."

"Seen evil," Frank Graham corrected.

"Seen evil," Billy corrected himself.

"A big difference between the two," Frank pointed out. "Now, start at the beginning and show us how far you can go."

Billy closed his eyes again and began: "Lord, thou hast been our dwelling place in all generations. Before the mountains were brought forth or ever thou hadst formed the earth and the world, even from everlasting to everlasting, thou art God." On and on he went, through the fifteenth verse, this time putting it correctly.

"Very good, son," Frank said. "You almost have it all. Now, read the sixteenth verse aloud for us."

Billy took the Bible and read: "Let thy work appear unto thy servants and thy glory unto their children."

"Good," Frank said. "Write it in your notebook and see that you have it memorized by tomorrow morning."

The questions passed around the table to each child, and each in turn recited Bible verses or gave catechism answers. At a quarter after eight, Morrow Graham said: "It's time to catch the bus."

The children went to their rooms to fetch their books and wraps. When they had gathered again at the kitchen door, Morrow Graham distributed their lunch boxes. Then they kissed her as they left the house. Standing at the door, she watched them go down to the road and wait for the school bus. Her eyes rested upon Billy and she frowned a little.

"Dear Lord," she prayed, "I know in my heart that the boy belongs to you and you want him in your service. Please do something to make him discover this for himself!"

iii

The high school department of the Sharon Hill country school offered a three-year course of eight months each. At 17, Billy was in the second year. His grades were average, rising or sinking depending on the extent of his extra-curricular interests. He could not let his grades fall too low because his mother and father paid too much attention to his report cards. They had extra occasions to know how he was doing: his father was chairman of the school board and his mother was president of the P. T. A.

But there were distractions nevertheless. In spring there was baseball, in autumn there was basketball, in winter there were books. Billy liked reading. Before he was ten he read through the *Billy Whiskers* series, and he enjoyed them so much that he convinced his father to buy a goat for him and he called it Billy. Charlie, the hired man, was amused and asked: "Is that such a good idea? People will wonder if you're named after the goat or the goat is named after you." Frank Graham observed: "There's really not much difference between the two of them."

Billy also liked the Tarzan books and read them all. Sometimes he got carried away by them and during his chores in the orchard he would swing from tree to tree and give what he thought was a good imitation of the Tarzan yell. These antics always terrified his sisters. Teasing them, he would become even more daring, until his mother called from the house to tell him to behave. A book he especially liked was the adventures of Marco Polo, and he re-read it often. The tales of the faraway places enchanted him: little did he know he would one day travel so widely himself that his trips would make Marco Polo's journeys look like the jaunts of a Venetian commuter. Billy's favorite reading position was stretched out on the floor of the Graham living-room in front of the fireplace. Invariably, he would start his reading while nibbling on a salted tomato and by the time he finished it he was too engrossed in his book to get up for another. The evening would end with him there on the floor, asleep over his book. With time, the spot became his favorite resting place. Even in his manhood, when he would return home and needed a nap, he would stretch out on the floor and the family would have to step over him to go about its business.

Cars were another distraction. Although he did not have a car of his own he frequently borrowed his father's and spent the evening racing along country roads and the suburban streets of Charlotte. He was a speed demon. Often his friends wondered if they would get home alive. At parties he quickly volunteered to chauffeur everybody home simply out of the joy of driving, and the brave accepted. He was careful, however, to slow down in the vicinity of his own home because he knew that if his father caught him speeding he would never get the car again.

Another distraction was girls. He was very popular with them; he knew this and enjoyed it. Scarcely a week passed without his announcing to his family: "Last night I met the prettiest girl I've ever seen." With that he would be off on another crush that, the family knew, would perhaps last a week. His parents never worried about him in such matters. In the first place, because the parade of the girls passed so rapidly, they were sure that he seldom went with any of them long enough to get serious. Secondly, they were confident that his home-training was sufficient to protect him from being dangerously carried away by any of his romances. They were right; his crushes were wholesome and harmless; the sheer number of them served to ward off complications. Years later while discussing his many teenage romances he said: "I never behaved improperly with any of the girls, nor did I even ever consider it." When the statement reached his mother she was surprised that he had found it necessary to utter it. "But I would be even more surprised if he had said anything else," she observed.

Morrow Graham knew her son better than he knew himself. She knew, too, the power of prayer, and she never completely abandoned her hope that Billy would respond to her prayers for his future. There were times when she discussed his future, nudging him towards the ministry.

"Suppose," she would ask, "you don't become a baseball player? What else would you want to be? Maybe a preacher?"

"Not *that*," Billy said firmly.

His firmness made his mother smile.

Circumstances in the Graham household enabled Billy to be familiar with the life a preacher led. The family was friendly with all the local clergy, and when evangelists worked in the area they were often invited to stay at the Graham home. Billy was thus on a first-name basis with a score of ministers. He evidently liked them as individuals, he was always ready to assist them in any way he could, but he showed no special interest in their profession. Patiently, Morrow Graham awaited the day when Billy would acquire the interest.

Meanwhile, Frank Graham was determined that Billy would not acquire any habits that might lead him in the wrong direction. One morning when Billy was eleven, Frank noticed that he had something in his mouth that made his cheeks bulge. "What in the world are you chewing on?" he asked.

"Tobacco," Billy said.

Frank's hand shot out and he gave Billy a ringing slap on the back of the head. The tobacco flew out of Billy's mouth and splattered across the barn. "Where did you get that stuff?" Frank Graham demanded.

"From Charlie," Billy said, gently rubbing his stinging neck.

"Don't you ever let me catch you using it again," warned Frank.

"What's wrong with it?" Billy asked. "Charlie uses it."

"I can't stop the hired help from using tobacco," said Frank, "but I can stop you. I don't want you to use tobacco in any form, hear?"

Billy heard, from that day on.

It was the same with alcohol. In 1933, when Prohibition was repealed, Frank Graham took both Billy and Catherine out to the barn. He said: "I suppose you've been reading in the papers that it's now going to be legal for people to drink alcohol."

"Yes, Daddy," Catherine said. Billy nodded.

"Well," said Frank, "I just want you to know that nobody in my family will be permitted to drink, regardless of the law. Alcohol is an evil thing and it will only get you into trouble. Do you understand?"

Catherine said: "Yes, Daddy." And Billy nodded again.

"Now," said Frank, "you're only human. You'll be seeing your friends drinking and you'll be curious to find out what it's like."

The two teenagers waited expectantly.

"I want you to find out now what it's like," said Frank. To the surprise of the two youngsters, Frank Graham took two bottles of beer from a shelf and opened them. "All right," he said, "I want you to drink these, drink them straight down without stopping." He gave a bottle to each of his children.

Catherine was astonished to find herself holding a bottle of beer in her hand; Billy fought a grin of amusement.

"Go ahead," said Frank Graham. "I want to watch you drink it down."

Catherine sipped the beer and grimaced. "It's bitter."

Billy gulped deep, then gasped. "It tastes like soap."

Frank Graham regarded the two bottles. "You haven't finished yet," he said. "Drink it all."

"Oh, Daddy!" Catherine pleaded. Billy held his bottle up to the light, saw how full it remained, and moaned.

"All of it," said Frank.

Meekly, the two teenagers obeyed. Finished, Billy said: "I think I'm going to vomit."

Frank Graham sat down triumphantly. "In the future when your friends tempt you to take a drink, you can tell them you've tried it and you don't like it. That is a good enough excuse for them," he said. "But I want you to have a better reason for yourselves. Drinking is wrong, and that's the reason you shouldn't do it. Is that clear?"

"Oh, yes," said Catherine, her face still distorted from the bitterness.

Billy asked: "I wonder how people get any fun out of it?"

"They don't," said Frank. "They just think it's smart."

"Well, I don't," said Billy, and that was the end of his adventures with alcohol.

Frank Graham felt he had wisely handled the problems of tobacco and alcohol with Billy. He realized that his orders of abstinence from both might make the boy look like a sissy to some of his friends, but he did not care about that. One thing was sure: Billy was no sissy. If anything, he was too much the contrary. In the process of growing up he had brought home more than his share of black eyes, each followed by complaints of community parents that Billy was too quick to settle his disputes with his fists. The disputes usually erupted on baseball diamonds over whether a pitch was a ball or strike or whether a runner was safe or out at first.

Also, at school Billy was inclined to be a little too rambunctious. At a P. T. A. meeting, one of his teachers told Frank Graham she occasionally had trouble making Billy settle down. Frank said: "You're the boss in the classroom. If Billy gets hard to handle, put a switch to him. That's what I would do at home." Learning this was enough to calm Billy—most of the time.

Billy was also a prankster. One of his favorite pranks involved the school bus. On leaving the bus at home, Billy would go around to the rear and turn off the valve that led to the fuel tank. The driver would manage to proceed a hundred yards before the motor died; he would know then that Billy was up to his tricks. He also enjoyed depositing harmless garden snakes into the chicken feed for his sisters to find when they did their chores. Billy's best friend was Grady Wilson, a neighboring farmboy, and their efforts to outdo each other at practical jokes kept their teachers and families in constant turmoil.

Aware of all these things, Frank Graham was not overly perturbed by any charges of unmanliness that Billy might face because he would not smoke or drink. But Frank knew how the boys might taunt his son, and he wondered how long Billy would endure until he felt it necessary to prove his masculinity. As far as Frank Graham was concerned, there was only one thing that Billy had to prove: that he was a creature of God, bound by the love of God to live as God desired. This, however, was something that Billy would first have to discover for himself. Discovering it, he would not have to prove anything to anybody; he would merely have to demonstrate his discovery in his daily life. Like Morrow, Frank Graham prayed that the day of discovery would come soon.

iv

That important day began the cold spring morning Billy had difficulty getting out of bed. There seemed to be nothing special about the day. As usual, Billy milked the cows and delivered his route and returned home for breakfast and the morning Bible lesson. With Catherine and Melvin, he went to the road to catch the school bus. Again as usual, he sat with Grady Wilson, and with their pranks and teasing they kept the bus in an uproar all the way to school. After lunch, the two boys practiced baseball with other members of the school team, and after school they worked out for another hour. Because most of the players were the sons of farmers and therefore had chores to do, they soon piled into cars to go home to work. Grady and Billy were in the same car.

Grady asked: "You going to the tent-meeting tonight, Bill?"

Billy had forgotten about it. He said: "No, I don't think so."

"Why not? It might be fun."

Billy shrugged. "Sometimes Mordecai Ham is too much fun."

The attitude was shared by many. Mordecai Ham was a popular evangelist whose convictions and services were extremely Fundamentalist. For the more sedate denominations he was at times a bit too violent, a bit too noisy. For this reason, he was considered rather controversial; his arrival was not widely welcomed, and when the calmer Christians attended his services they went more to be amused than to worship. The Grahams were among those who preferred to await the visits of less demonstrative evangelists.

Grady said: "Let's go anyway, Bill. We haven't got anything else to do tonight."

"I'll think about it," Billy offered.

He did not think about it until dinner, when the subject of the evening's occupations came up in the family talk. He decided that moment that Grady might be right: Mordecai Ham might be fun, and besides there was nothing else to do.

"I'm going to the meeting," Billy said.

Frank Graham glanced at Billy appraisingly. "Mordecai Ham's meeting?"

"Yes. Some of the fellows thought we'd all go in for a while."

Frank looked back at his plate. He would have preferred that Billy didn't go, and yet he couldn't advise his son not to attend a religious service. He resigned himself to the fact that although there might not be much good achieved at the meeting at least there would be no harm done.

Morrow Graham had her own suspicions. She said: "I hope you're not going just to sit there and yell and holler and cause a rumpus?"

"Oh, no," Billy answered, too quickly.

"If you want to worship, worship," said Morrow, "but don't go just to ridicule Mr. Ham. He means well, even if his way isn't ours."

"I wouldn't ridicule a preacher," Billy said.

"See you behave, then," Morrow said.

A few minutes before eight, Billy drew his father's car to a stop in the parking lot adjacent to Mordecai Ham's big tent. Men and women who, by their dress and manner, were recognizably mountain people who had migrated to Charlotte, N. C. flocked inside. "There go the screamers," Grady observed.

"I've got orders to behave," Billy said in warning.

Grady smiled. "What if the 'spirit' hits you?"

"I come from good Presbyterians; we *are* the 'spirit'." And he returned Grady's smile with a teasing grin of his own. "Let's go in."

They found seats near the back, on the aisle. The tent was almost filled, and among the crowd they recognized several friends. Three boys from school saw them and waved, their eyes bright with rascality. Billy nodded knowingly. He was suddenly uncomfortable, aware that his intentions for coming were not entirely noble. He wished the service would start.

At last, a few minutes past eight, it did. Mordecai Ham stepped to the platform and was greeted by a rustle of excitement. His rich voice was calm and warming.

"Welcome, brothers and sisters," he said. "Welcome in the name of the Lord."

A man in the audience called: "It is good to be here, Brother Ham."

Several people said: "Amen."

"Shall we," said Ham, "shall we invite the spirit to join us by singing a few sacred songs?" He picked up a hymnal. "Let us begin with 'Shall We Gather At The River?'"

They progressed from one hymn to the next, and with each the rhythm grew more sprightly, more specific. Soon there was a tense impatience in the air. Billy could feel it; so could Grady. "Fireworks any minute," Grady said. Billy nodded and sent his alert glance over the crowd. It was the "fireworks" that many people disliked —the emotional explosions that made the worshipers scream and writhe and weep. Billy disliked them; knowing they were about to begin made him uneasy.

"Very good, very good," Mordecai Ham said to the crowd. "Now Brother Miller has a word for you."

Ham stepped aside and turned the platform over to one of his assistants. Everybody knew Brother Miller was going to talk about money, which he did in a heated, well-plotted ten minute speech on the high cost of bringing the meetings to Charlotte. His own conversion, he said, had taken place at a tent-meeting, just as surely others would be converted tonight, and if the people wanted Brother Ham to continue to come to them, saving their souls, they would have to share the expense of it. His point was valid, it was dramatically put, and it was effective.

Mordecai Ham returned. He stood there a silent moment, gazing at his audience, waiting as wallets were put away and purses were snapped shut and the people settled down. Then he said quietly: "Praise the Lord, brothers and sisters."

The cries came back: "Praise the Lord, Brother Ham! The Lord be with you, Brother! Hallelujah!"

Ham let the cries fade, then he leaned forward and declared in a loud voice: "Praise the Lord, brothers and sisters, because you are all sinners and you are doomed to fire and damnation!"

A groan of pain went through the tent.

"You are damned because of your sins!" Ham shouted. He changed his tone to knowing patience. "Oh, don't think that you are fooling the Lord. He knows what you're doing. He sees you every minute. He sees into your mind and into your heart and He knows all the evil that is festering there. You can fool your wife or your husband or your neighbors or your friends, but you can't fool the Lord. He knows you as the sinner you are and He won't let you get away with it, not for a minute. You are sinners, sinners, and you know as well as the Lord knows it. The Bible says, 'Lo, even if I go to the ends of the earth you are there.' The Lord is there, brothers and sisters, the Lord is with you wherever you go, whatever you do, and He is angry with you because you don't think about Him enough. You turn your back on Him, you shut your eyes to Him, you close your heart to Him. Do you think He is going to let you get away with that?"

Again came the cries: "Hallelujah, Brother! Save us, Brother." A woman sent out a piercing scream.

Ham went on, his voice loud and challenging, his words sharp with accusations and threats.

Billy Graham listened, uncomfortable and aloof at first, then interested and deeply concerned. He found himself wincing each time Ham cried: "You are a sinner." As Ham continued for half an hour, Billy heard his inner voice declare: "He is talking about me." Billy stiffened in his chair, his hands gripping his knees, his eyes unmoving. No longer did he pay attention to the cries of the people around him, the sobs of women, the self-recriminating shouts of the men, the spasms of some person shaken with remorse. He stared straight ahead at Mordecai Ham and listened, repeating again and again to himself: "He is talking about me."

Mordecai Ham went on:

"The Bible says, 'He who is not with me is against me.' That's what Jesus said. Brothers and sisters, how do you measure up to that? Are you with Jesus or against Him? Do you just give Him lip service or do you really love Him? Do you really let Him rule your life or do you just think of Him on Sunday mornings and when some preacher comes around with a tent? Answer that question, brothers and sisters. Let me hear you answer that question."

The answers came: "Show us the way to the Lord, Brother Ham! Make us love Him! Oh, Brother, save us from hellfire!"

Billy remained silent, his thoughts on his personal life. Certainly religion was a living thing for him each day: his parents saw to that. But now Billy wondered how much of religion was merely habit. Did he learn his daily Bible verse out of love for the Lord or because his father expected it of him? Did he take part in the family prayers out of a desire to worship or because he had grown up in a house where prayers were regular practice? Wasn't it true that he thought more often of baseball and cars and girls than he did about God? Wasn't it also true that he had come to the tent-meeting more to see a show than to hear the Word? Was he a hypocrite? Was he possibly now seeing himself for the first time, seeing himself as God saw him?

Mordecai Ham's voice rose. "Do you really love the Lord? Do you think about Him at the moment of temptation? Do you let Him guide everything you think and do? Have you given yourself completely to Him?"

Billy whispered: "Not yet, but I will."

Grady said: "What?"

Billy shook his head to silence Grady.

The tent grew noisy: the moment of decision was approaching.

Mordecai Ham said: "All right, now, brothers and sisters. The time has come. You've been sitting there for an hour listening to me beg you to stop sinning and walk at the side of the Lord. I can stand here and beg you to do it, but you are the only one who can make yourself do it. Will you? Will you become a child of Jesus? Think about it. Look into your hearts for the answer. Will you love the Lord? You know you should. You know you must. Decide now. Decide now and then show Jesus that you are His. Come forward, brothers and sisters, come forward and give witness of your decision. Come on up here, brothers and sisters, stand up here with me and let's pray together. Come on up here and give yourselves to the Lord!"

Billy got to his feet. Grady Wilson was surprised. "Going home, Bill?" he asked.

Billy did not answer.

Grady rose, expecting to follow Billy out of the tent. Instead, Billy made his way with slow, determined steps down the aisle to Mordecai Ham. Others slipped into the aisle to join Billy, but he was unaware of them. When he reached the front, he stood a little aside, he folded his hands in front of him, he lowered his head, and he listened to the steady, heavy beating of his heart.

He had gone home. He had gone home, indeed.

Chapter II

In an hour the news had raced to all of Billy's friends. Billy Graham had been converted. There was a great deal of surprise and astonishment. Billy? Converted? What did it mean?

Youngsters who were closest to Billy were certain he had few if any sins in his personal life to renounce. They knew him to be a healthy, wholesome, uncomplicated teenager whose habits and attitudes reflected the exemplary Christian atmosphere of the Graham home. They knew that he was already a religious boy, and they wondered what in the world he had to be converted from—or to.

Actually Billy's conversion was not the usual abandonment of evil ways: his home environment, his chores and jobs, his school, his carefree enjoyment of his friends, his love of sports and speed had sheltered him from evil. His conversion, then, was an expreience in discovery. A casual faith became a throbbing faith. An acknowledgment of Christ became a specific awareness of Him. Habitual prayers became vibrant prayers. The Holy Writ of the Bible became the Holy Will of God. Daily life became the daily adventure of carrying out God's Will.

That this should have happened to Billy so quickly, so

vividly, in the frantic atmosphere of the climaxing moments of a tent-meeting was not unusual. God had to knock Paul off his horse to make him recognize his error in persecuting the first Christians. Billy's error had been merely that his religion, however sincere, had been skin-deep. At a tent-meeting Billy had attended mostly to be amused an evangelist found the right words to pierce through years of habit and routine and make Billy's religion the most vital factor of his life. It was an experience that could only be accepted by those who witnessed it and appreciated only by those who had undergone it themselves. It was like a second birth, a second baptism. It was the moment of new life.

Driving home, Grady and Billy were silent. This had been a big night for Grady, too. He tried to explain it this way: "I was sitting there, Bill, with this feeling growing inside me, wanting to go up front and say out loud that I'm a Christian, but I was scared to death of moving, scared I'd make myself look foolish in front of all the guys. Then you got up. I thought you wanted to leave. But I watched you head down the aisle, right down there to ole Mordecai, and I said to myself, thank God, thank God, now I can go forward, too, and everything will be all right. It was really something, Bill."

"It sure was," Billy agreed.

Grady said: "Bill, I've been thinking. I think tonight changed my whole life. I think now I'm going to become a preacher, too."

"Yeah? That's swell, Grady."

"What about you? Has going forward changed you?"

"Of course, Grady, but I'm not sure how much yet. One thing I am sure of," said Billy. "From now on I'm leaving everything to Christ. I'm sure He'll let me know what He wants me to do."

Grady grinned a little. "Suppose He wants you in a pulpit instead of in the big leagues?"

Billy detected the tease. "It'll be the big leagues, buddy, one way or the other."

With the exception of the night-light in the kitchen, the Graham house was dark when Billy reached home shortly after ten o'clock. He put the car away, then entered the back door. He felt a little hungry and looked into the refrigerator for something to eat, deciding at last to settle for a glass of milk. He leaned against the kitchen sink, a half smile on his face as he thought of Grady's somber concern for him. Certainly Billy did not feel somber. On the contrary, he could not remember when he had felt so light of heart. He finished the milk, rinsed the glass and put it away, then went upstairs to his room.

As he prepared for bed he noticed the book he had been reading and considered giving it a few minutes as he fell asleep, but then he remembered the late hour and that he would have to be up at three to milk and he decided he'd better get to sleep as fast as he could. He had just climbed into bed and turned out the lamp when he heard a knock at his door. He asked: "Yes?"

The door opened and Billy recognized his mother's silhouette.

"Yes, Ma?"

"Are you all right, son?" Morrow Graham asked.

"Sure, Ma. Why?"

"Mrs. Hamner stopped by; she was at the meeting."

"Oh."

"She told us what happened."

Billy waited.

Morrow Graham said: "I'm glad, Billy Frank."

"So am I, Ma."

"Your father is happy about it, too." They looked at each other silently in the darkness. She said: "It's an important thing you did tonight; I've been praying for it for a long time."

"I know."

"I've been praying for a lot of things for you."

He knew she was referring to the ministry, and he laughed softly. "I'm going to have to watch out for you: your prayers are always answered."

She let him enjoy teasing her, then she said: "I hope they are, son, as far as you're concerned."

ii

In the early morning there was not much time for talk. As they did every morning, Billy, Melvin, Frank Graham and Charlie went about their work with quiet preoccupation, each too busy to chat. It was not until he was driving into the city to begin his deliveries that Billy had time to think about himself.

He had, he knew, changed in a definite way, and yet he could not identify the change. He felt happy, but then he had never been a morose young man; he felt dedicated and purposeful, but then he had never been a drifter; he felt confident, but then he had rarely been uncertain. He did not feel a new surge of piety, and he wondered if he should. God had suddenly become very real and personal to him, and Billy thought that this new sensation of discovery should be accompanied by some kind of spiritual ecstasy. But it was not. Simply, he felt secure, warm and unusually happy. Several times he caught himself smiling at nothing in particular, which then made him laugh at himself. He shook his head, amused. It was good to be alive.

He knew for certain he was going to become a minister. How this would please his mother. And yet he would not do it merely for that reason. He had to become a minister; that was all there was to it. He had to serve God, specifically, directly, intimately. Surely there were many like himself, millions, perhaps, who needed only a singular spiritual experience to draw them closer to God, and Billy now felt it was his responsibility to provide the occasion of that experience, if it was at all possible. The decision, he was confident, was not entirely his own; God's Will was a factor in it, and it would be wrong for him to resist it. All that was necessary now was for him to take the first steps: God would provide the way.

The first steps were taken at breakfast. When the meal was over, Frank Graham, as usual, reached for the Bible for the morning's lessons. There was a silent moment, full of waiting. Billy sensed the family expected some remarks from him.

He cleared his throat and looked down at his plate. "Something happened to me last night," he said, knowing that all of them knew it. "At Mordecai Ham's meeting, I felt impelled to go forward and declare myself for Christ."

No one spoke.

Billy added: "I'm very happy that I did it."

Frank Graham studied his son. "We are, too," he said at last.

More waiting.

Billy said: "I know my life has changed, but I'm not sure how. I am sure of something else, though. When I finish high school, I'd like to study for the ministry."

There was a stir of approval around the table. Morrow Graham's eyes filled with tears. More waiting.

Billy looked at his father, then at the Bible. "Do you want me to start this morning?"

"All right."

Billy began to recite the Ninetieth Psalm, and this morning the words were full of meaning for him.

He was apprehensive about school. He was afraid his friends would expect too great a change in him, and he didn't want that. To guard against it at home, Billy made a point of giving Catherine's long hair a sharp tug as they walked down to the bus.

She cried: "Billy Frank, you stop that!" And in return he grabbed one of her schoolbooks and sent it on a forward-pass to Melvin.

Boarding the bus, Billy said: "Good morning, Mr. Shaw. You've got a flat tire."

Startled, the driver exclaimed: "I have?" And he darted out for a look. He was back in a moment, frowning with disgust, and he said: "I was expecting better of you this morning, Billy."

Grady Wilson was relieved to see that Billy remained his old teasing self. As Billy slid into the seat beside Grady he noticed in front the girl on whom Grady had an unrequited crush. Billy poked Grady with his elbow and asked loudly: "Grady, what's this I hear about you and

Lucy Carter running off last night and getting married?"

Grady blushed. The girl turned around and announced haughtily: "I wouldn't marry Grady Wilson if he was the last boy on earth."

Billy grinned back at her. "Better not wait 'til the competition gets any tougher for you than it is!"

Lucy said: "Oh!" And she turned away.

At school, Billy perceived that everybody was watching him appraisingly. To overcome the discomfort of others, Billy made more jokes and teased more than he normally did. He realized that the moment would come soon enough when he would have to take a stand in front of his friends, but he wanted to postpone that moment until he felt he had the right words to say.

After lunch, Billy joined other players of the school baseball team for a practice game. He was in excellent form. He hit well and his fielding was exceptional. At one point he caught a fast line drive, then whipped the ball to second to catch the runner for a double-play. The quick play confused the teenage umpire and he called the runner safe.

Billy dashed to the infield. "What d'ya mean—safe? He was out by a mile!"

"I was safe," the runner called.

"That's right," the umpire said.

Billy slammed his glove onto the grass. "He's out! I'm tellin' you, he's out!"

The coach trotted to the growing cluster of players. "Hold it, hold it," he said. "I saw the play. The runner is out. Everybody calm down."

Defensively, the umpire said: "He looked safe to me."

"Yeah?" said Billy, calming. "Well, get yourself some glasses, you blind bat."

The second-baseman laughed. "Attaboy, Billy, fight it out. This is a ball game, not a heebie-jeebie tent-meeting. Boy, I was worried you were really serious last night."

This was the moment.

Billy looked at the boy, ignoring the others gathered around. "Don't get the wrong impression, Jimmy," Billy said soberly. "I was serious last night, more serious than

I've ever been about anything. I've declared myself for Jesus, not just for last night but for my whole life. But what do you expect me to do—go and live in the middle of the desert?"

Jimmy was taken aback and tried to soothe Billy. "Okay," he said, "okay, Preacher, okay. That's fine with me. You can go to tent-meetings every night."

Billy's mood changed; a grin tugged at his lips. "I may just do that. And you want to know something, Jimmy? You're coming with me tonight."

The boys laughed. Jimmy said: "The heck I will!"

Billy said: "The heck you won't. I'll be at your house for you at seven-thirty."

The boys laughed again and Jimmy groaned.

The double-play had retired the sides. During preparations for the next inning, someone asked: "Who's up first?"

The scorekeeper checked his papers. "The Preacher's up first."

The team-captain called to Billy: "Hey, Preacher, you're up first."

Billy nodded and went to choose a bat, lowering his head so that the others could not see his amusement at his new nickname. "Well," he said to himself, "I'd better get used to it."

iii

The next year passed quickly, and Billy was very happy during it. He commented to his parents that even the leaves on the trees seemed to look greener to him. Having a definite purpose now, a definite goal, he applied himself more to his studies and earned his highest marks. He spent less time racing about in cars, more time at home, reading on the floor. In addition to the family's regular religious practices, Billy took on private Bible reading for a half-hour everyday. The year matured him, quieting him considerably. Nevertheless, he thought it was only fitting that, on his last day at Sharon Hills High

School, he should, as he had done so frequently, switch off the valve to the fuel tank on the schoolbus, and when it sputtered to a halt a few yards down the road he let out a victorious Tarzan yell.

He decided to begin his studies for the ministry at Bob Jones College, at Cleveland, Tennessee. The choice was indicative. Bob Jones had been a famous evangelist, having started his own career at the mild age of 15, at the turn of the century. He had preached all over the world, written many books, and he was especially interested in the spiritual development of the young. In 1928, Jones opened his Tennessee school, which was primarily intended to be a training ground for future evangelists.

Billy Graham, then, wanted to become an evangelist. It was, he knew, a decision that would mean hard work, constant travel, few personal roots. It would mean long separations from home, from his family and friends, from all the things and people he had grown up among and loved so dearly. But he was ready for that. He felt a vibrant desire to share his discovery of God with as many people as possible, an urge to tell everyone in the world what he now knew and what they could know for themselves: God's distinct, personal, stirring love and its profound effect on daily life.

Having chosen his school, Billy faced the problem of paying for it. Actually, this was his own idea. The Graham dairy was more than successful enough for Billy's parents to afford to pay for his education, but he insisted on earning his own way. With the exception of the money he was paid for playing baseball, Billy had never been on a salary. He had not been paid for his work at the dairy nor for his route, but he did not expect to be paid for that. The dairy, after all, supported the family, and as a member of the family he felt he was merely doing his share. Baseball provided him with spending money in the summer; in winter, he asked his mother for money when he needed it. A nickel or a dime was usually enough to get him through an evening; if he intended to treat a girl to a soda he might ask for a quarter. Requesting or accepting such small sums did not embarrass him nor did he ever resent it. Even before his conversion he was completely free of pride, free of any necessity to show off, to a girl or his friends, that, at the height of the Depression years, his family was comparatively well off.

Thus on leaving high school in 1937, he went into Charlotte to look for a job. Grady Wilson went with him.

There were few jobs available, and for those that were there was always a line of married men with families after them. Several days of trying had Billy and Grady wondering if they would ever get on a payroll. Their youth was against them, so was their inexperience, so was their admission that they intended to quit the jobs in the fall to go to college. In time, they realized that their best hope was to take jobs that paid only a commission —selling jobs, where they would be hired because of their eagerness and kept on because of their success. They found such jobs with the Fuller Brush Company.

"Selling brushes?" Catherine Graham asked increduously at dinner that night. "How can you make a living selling brushes?"

"People need brushes," Billy said in defense. "Mother, don't you need brushes every once in a while?"

"Yes," Morrow Graham said, "but don't get the idea I'm going to stock up now just to help you get rid of your supply."

The idea had occurred to him. "Of course not," he said, dismissing it. "But the point is that women do need brushes and now I'm going to see that they get the chance to buy them."

Melvin was interested. "Charlotte's a big city, Billy Frank. Lots of women will buy from you in Charlotte."

"I won't be working in Charlotte," said Billy. "The senior men get the big cities. Grady and I will work small towns and rural areas. We'll probably have to go on the road." He enjoyed the prospect.

Morrow Graham did not. "You and Grady going to be working together all the time?"

"The same areas, at least."

"Well, that's good. I wouldn't want you traipsing all over the country by yourself."

"I can take care of myself," Billy said.

"Just the same. . . ." It was unpleasant to think he would be away.

He was not away too often. Usually his sales team left the Charlotte areas in the early morning to spend the day within a 25-mile range of the city, and they were back in the late evening. Occasionally it was necessary to stay away overnight, and during the whole summer they were rarely required to be on the road more than two or three days. There was no reason to worry. Not only was Grady always with him, but Billy was now so intently dedicated to his future in the ministry that, as at home, he continued his daily Bible studies. He was, furthermore, highly successful at selling the brushes and was called upon to explain his technique to other salesmen. "I believe in the product," he said. "Otherwise I don't think I could do it." This was another example of his sincerity in all things.

The summer passed quickly. Soon it was September, time to begin college. Cleveland was about 150 miles from Charlotte and the traffic between the two cities was steady; it would be simple for Billy to hitchhike home for weekends and holidays. Although he would be separated from the family by a greater distance than before and for longer periods, his sheltered life as a student eased his parents' concern. Moreover, the fact that he was on the threshold of his life in the service of God was a great consolation to them.

After a few weeks, however, Frank and Morrow Graham perceived that Billy was not entirely happy at Bob Jones College. He had no specific complaint; the school was fine, the faculty was sympathetic, the students were friendly, the studies interesting. Nevertheless Billy seemed dissatisfied. He said nothing definite, but his attitude was plain.

"I wonder," Frank ventured to his wife after one of

Billy's visits home, "if this means Billy feels he might not be cut out for the ministry."

"He will have to decide that for himself," said Morrow. "No matter how much we want him to be a minister, we mustn't try to force him into it unless he is sure."

"I don't think we could," Frank said. "Billy Frank is too honest with himself to go ahead with this unless he was sure he was meant for it. If he has any doubts...."

"We should pray that he does the right thing," Morrow said. "Whatever it is, he will let us know when he is ready."

The term had almost ended before Billy said anything. At dinner one night he remarked: "I don't think I'll be going back to college."

Morrow Graham did not look up from her plate, but said quietly: "Oh?"

Frank asked: "Anything wrong?"

"Oh, no," Billy said quickly, and his tone was so clearly innocent that they knew he was not hiding anything.

Disappointment welled in Morrow Graham. "Have you any plans?" she asked carefully.

"Yes, as a matter of fact I do," said Billy. They waited as he took another bite of food. Then: "I think I'll transfer to the Florida Bible Institute, at Tampa."

Frank and Morrow exchanged a quick glance. Frank said: "You're still going on to the ministry?"

The question surprised Billy, then made him smile. "So that's why you've both been so sullen? What a pair you are! Of course I'm going on. What made you think I wasn't?"

His parents were smiling now. Frank said: "We weren't sure that you were sure."

"You've been so noncommittal lately," Morrow said.

"Well, I am sure," Billy said with confidence. "In all my life I've only been surer of one other thing—that I've got wonderful parents who worry in silence about me too much."

Obliquely Morrow began: "We didn't want to interfere...."

Billy laughed with love and knowing. "And those prayers of yours—I suppose you wouldn't call them interference?"

All their faces shone with understanding and joy.

iv

Billy chose to transfer to the Florida Bible Institute simply because he felt an attraction to it. In terms of religious vocations, experiencing the attraction could well be accepted as a manifestation of the Will of God. As soon as Billy entered the school, he was comfortable in it, at home and at ease. He was able to apply himself to his studies more intensely than ever before. There was a new confidence about him: he was a young man who knew he was on the right road. The Florida Bible Institute was a Baptist institution, but Billy's Presbyterian parents did not make an issue of it. After all, it was Billy's life and Billy's vocation, and they felt he should proceed in both as he chose.

At the Institute, Billy adhered to a decision he had made on leaving high school: he insisted on earning his own way. The Tampa area attracted many tourists; Billy caddied for them on local golf courses. He discovered that he liked the game and taught himself to play it. Lacking a professional tutor, he started out by taking the wrong grip on the stick, developing a cross-handed grasp that took much of his natural power out of his swing. It wasn't until years later, when golf was the only exercise for which he had time, that he corrected his grip and improved his game so that he could play with the best golfers without embarrassment.

Billy also washed dishes at the Institute, earning twenty cents an hour. Unlike some of the other students, Billy did not resent his humble chore. On the contrary, he made a game of it, competing with himself to set daily records for speed, cleanliness and quantity. He worked five hours a day at the dishes, keeping five students busy drying. The little free time he had left Billy used to earn money shining shoes in Tampa. Once again he was free of the pride that kept others from the street-corner job. He was making himself independent, he was not being a burden to his family, moreover he was having fun.

He loved the Institute. Its atmosphere was freer than Bob Jones College, its discipline freer, and its president, Dr. William T. Watson, was a deeply spiritual man who had a keen insight into the hearts and minds of the young seminarians. Most of the professors were, like Dr. Watson, practicing ministers, which gave their courses an important practicality. Often there were lectures by visiting evangelists, active men who knew all the problems in the field and gave the students the benefit of their vital experience. Billy could not wait for the day when he could join their ranks.

In a way, the day came much sooner than he expected. Each summer he paired up with Grady Wilson to resume his career as a Fuller Brush salesman. They were both by now trusted and skilled employees; the company let them wander wherever they chose. Eager to accumulate money for school, both boys took every advantage to save a dollar. It was while they were at Monroe, North Carolina, that they encountered Jimmie Johnson, a young evangelist who stayed at the Graham home when he worked near Charlotte. Johnson agreed to help the boys save hotel rent by letting them sleep in his tent-tabernacle.

Actually they slept on the ground, in the sawdust in front of the platform where Jimmie Johnson preached each night. Neatly folded on nearby chairs were their clothes; their big cases of brushes served as partitions to block out the morning sun that poured through the broad entrances and to hide the sleeping salesmen from the eyes of anyone who might wander into the tent early in the day. The accommodations were primitive, but they were free so they were appreciated.

One morning when Jimmie Johnson came to wake the boys for breakfast, he said: "I'm going over to visit the prisoners in the jail this morning. Care to come along?"

Billy Graham had never seen the inside of a jail before.

Billy said: "That should be interesting. Let's go along, Grady." Grady was willing.

The hardened prisoners groaned their displeasure when the jailer announced that an evangelist was coming in to see them. Jimmie Johnson was accustomed to the rude reception. Undaunted, he stood in the middle of the corridor of cells and told the men quite simply that if they would only give their lives to the Lord they would never be in jails again. The rules for purposeful living that Jesus offered the world were, Johnson said, the only assurances of personal peace. If the prisoners would abide by them after they left jail they would discover a spiritual freedom that could guarantee an individual freedom the rest of their lives.

The prisoners were not impressed. Jimmie Johnson glanced down the corridor and saw Billy and Grady. Johnson said: "I have a young preacher-friend here who can tell you from his own experience what can happen to a man when he answers the call of the Lord. Billy, would you say a few words to these men?"

Astonded, Billy backed away. Then he saw the highly amused grin on Grady's face. Billy knew that Grady, on his own road to the ministry, had already preached to a congregation and that he was now enjoying his superiority at Billy's expense. Billy refused to let such a situation endure for long. Squaring his thin shoulders, he stepped to the middle of the corridor. He had noticed how the prisoners ignored Jimmie Johnson; he would not let them ignore him.

"Now you men listen to me," he said in a loud voice. "I'm going to tell you something that can change your whole futures. It is something that changed mine, so I know what I'm talking about. So stop lurking in your cells and turn around and listen to me."

His stern tone alarmed the prisoners. Puzzled, they moved closer to the bars and looked bewildered at the heated young man in front of them.

Aware that he had their attention, Billy said: "I was a sinner. Never mind the details, but I can tell you right now that I was a sinner and an ungrateful bum. I thought only about myself and what I wanted for myself. didn't care that—" he snapped his fingers—"for God, he Bible, my family or friends. I just wanted to see to it hat I had a good time. Well, having a good time almost anded me where you are. But let me tell you what happened. Let me tell you what happened to me one night n Charlotte." He began to pace up and down the corridor. "I accepted Jesus as my savior. That's what I did. And ou can take my word for it that He changed my life. Overnight I changed from a sinner and a bum to a man of peace and joy. And Jesus can do this for you." He pointed at one man and then another. "He will take away your sins as he took away my sins. He will give you an inner peace that will straighten out your whole lives. All you have to do is let Him enter your hearts. He wants to, but you are locking Him out. If that wasn't true, you wouldn't be where you are now. Let Jesus enter your hearts. He died on the cross so that you could have new life. Take the new life now. He wants to give it to you. Love Jesus. Loving Him is the only thing that will save you."

With that, Billy turned quickly, picked up his sample case and hiked dramatically out of the jail. Outside, he leaned weakly against the building, his chest heaving, his heart pounding. After a moment Grady and Jimmie Johnson joined him.

"Well," said Johnson, "that was quite a sermon, my young friend."

"Was it all right?" Billy asked, struggling to get his breath. "It was my first one."

"I know," said Grady, smiling broadly. "You know, with a little practice you might turn into a pretty good preacher!"

Chapter III

Then love came along.

Billy was 20. Everything seemed to be going well for him. His mere presence in the Florida Bible Institute indicated his intentions for the future: the ministry. True his actual plans were vague, and when called upon to tell anyone precisely how he would occupy himself in the years to come he could not do so. He was like a young man who said he was interested in science but could not say exactly which science. But he was not perturbed by this. The years would take care of themselves. Billy expected he would become an itinerant evangelist, and yet just how this would come about he did not know: God would tell him at the proper time.

All this, however, was not enough for a young lady who became important to Billy when he was 20. She was a student at the Institute, attractive, popular, intelligent, devout. Billy met her through Wendell Phillips, his roommate, and in a short time Billy was telling Wendell that, as far as he was concerned, he had met the girl he was going to marry.

The girl seemed to return Billy's feelings. They became close friends; other students looked upon them as being paired off. The time came when Billy felt it proper to consider himself engaged and he said so to Wendell

Wendell was delighted. "Okay, send her the flowers."

It was a campus tradition. Because most of the students were poor, engagement rings were out of the question. However, when the moment of understanding came between a young couple the boy offered the girl a bouquet of flowers, part of which she wore as a corsage. Her acceptance of the flowers indicated her acceptance of him.

Thereafter, the boy sent the girl a corsage for every school event, which she wore as a sign to other young men that she was spoken for.

Ordinarily the flowers cost a quarter. His heart full of love, Billy spent fifty cents on the first corsage he was to present to the girl. He was in for the shock of his life.

"It's very sweet of you, Bill," the girl said, looking at the flowers he held out to her, "but I can't accept it."

Billy was stunned. "You can't? Why not?"

The moment was uncomfortable for both of them. The girl said: "I don't think you're the man for me, Bill."

"You certainly haven't given me that impression," said Billy. "You know that I love you; I thought that you loved me. We've been spending an awful lot of time together."

"I wanted to get to know you better," the girl said.

Hurt, Billy said bitterly: "Well, I hope you found out whatever it was you wanted to know." Then he realized he had been cruel. He turned away. "I'm sorry. It's just that I thought you cared for me."

"I do," said the girl. "I'm very fond of you, Bill. But not that way." She looked at the flowers. Then she said: "The truth is, Bill, I don't think you're ready to get serious with any girl, particularly me."

"Why not? What's wrong with me?"

She had apparently thought it out. "You're immature," she said. "You're a drifter. You're irresponsible. I've listened to you talk and I don't see anything in your plans of a clear, Christian purpose."

"Just why do you think I'm at this school?" Billy asked quietly.

"Oh, Billy," she said impatiently, "lots of students here don't go on into church work."

"I intend to."

"As an evangelist?" She disapproved, evidently. "What kind of life is that? Would you expect your wife to be traveling with you all the time? What kind of homelife would you have? How could you expect to raise children?" She shook her head. "No, I'd want more security than that."

There was nothing more to discuss. Billy walked away. He walked for hours before he realized he was still carrying the flowers. He let them drop into a gutter.

He was depressed for days, suffering a period of doubt and puzzlement. Wendell Phillips was home on sick leave; Billy wrote him: "All the stars have fallen out of my sky. There is nothing to live for."

Wendell replied quickly with the deepest consolations. He quoted from Romans 8:28: "And we know that all things work together for good to them that love God, to them who are called according to His purpose."

Billy tried to apply the quotation, but his pain was too great. This was his first serious disappointment and he needed time to adjust to it. For a while he wondered if he really belonged in the ministry. He considered leaving the Institute, but he suspected such action appealed to him because it offered an escape from the girl's presence on the campus. He did not know what to do with himself; he had no idea where to turn.

It was on another of his lonely night walks that his mind cleared. Pondering on his past life, he remembered the tent-meeting and Mordecai Ham. He remembered his joy that night, the exhilaration that had kept him afloat for days and set the course of his future. The thought occurred to him that a disappointment in love had overshadowed the zeal that had brought him to the Institute in the first place. Unrequited love had detoured him from the very purpose he had declared so openly to his friends at the baseball game the day after his conversion.

He stopped in his tracks. "What a fool I've been!" he said aloud. "What a hypocrite! Here I've pledged my life to Christ and now I'm about to walk out on Him just because some girl doesn't love me! The Lord is all that matters. I tried to tell that to some prisoners in a jail; now the first time I'm really tested I don't live up to it myself!"

He hurried back to the Institute and wrote Wendell Phillips:

"I have settled it once and for all with the Lord. No

girl or friends or anything shall ever come first in my life. I have resolved that the Lord Jesus Christ shall have all of me. I care not what the future holds. I have determined to follow Him at all costs."

ii

He became a different young man. The change in him was so immediately noticeable that his professors remarked about it. His studies came easier than they ever had; he began to shine in his classes. He was especially interested in the class on preaching. This, he knew, would be a vital part of his career as an evangelist: it was important that he should develop into a good speaker.

To prepare himself, he gave added attention to the sermons he heard at school and at the various services he attended in the Tampa area. Available to him in the Institute library were the published sermons of the world's great preachers. He read them all, then he read them again—aloud. He went to the extent of copying down the sermons in order to acquire the rhythm of them, their balances and emphases. He even memorized some of them.

In the preaching class, the students usually spoke from a few notes or relied on memorizing the high points of what they planned to say. For Billy this was not enough. He composed his student-sermons on paper in full—regardless of the precious study-time this took away from his other courses. Having written them out, he memorized them, and he was thus able to go before his fellow-students thoroughly perpared. Preaching, he felt, was too vital an opportunity to get across the message of Christ for anyone to take it casually.

He gave his sermons verve and drama, not only in the choice of words and thoughts but in the presentation. Ordinarily he practiced the sermons in his room, which meant that his voice went ringing down the halls until other students hollered: "Hey, Billy, calm down! How can we study with all that racket?"

Determined, he decided he would have to find some other place to practice. He went out into the woods, along the banks of the Hillsboro River, and practiced there. Many were the afternoons that he climbed atop of a cypress stump and let his clear, strong voice shatter the woodland quiet in a plea for sinners to step forward and accept Christ. Startled birds winged down for a look at him; muskrats peeked at him over the river bank and then darted back when his gestures grew too flamboyant; bear cubs, attracted by the noise, shinnied up trees for a better look at this creature who had come into their domain with such disturbing energy; fishermen in their boats paused as they rowed by, wondering if the police should be notified of the madman shouting to himself in the woods. Billy ignored all of them.

The only doubts he now had about himself were typical of a man like Billy Graham. Humbly, he didn't think he was worthy of the task he had taken on. He felt he was not a good enough preacher for the ministry and never would be, that he lacked the intellectuality, the sensitivity and the drive required of a minister, and he feared that when he completed his studies and was ready to take on his work no church would have him. Paradoxically, these nagging doubts were normal in any sincere aspirant for the ministry, for a prerequisite to an effective ministry was the recognition that a man alone was helpless: only with God's specific help could he achieve anything worth while in the spiritual realm. Nevertheless, the doubts were often enough to drive a man away from the ministry and—oddly enough—the retreats were usually for the best. It was only when a student threw himself helplessly at God's feet and offered himself to be used by God in any way He chose that he acquired the kind of faith that would make him useful.

Billy suffered these torments of doubts even when he was most determined to become a preacher. After a day's hard study, he would stroll alone at night, wondering about himself, wanting so strongly to serve God but unsure that God wanted him as a servant.

Pondering about himself, Billy said aloud one night:

"Am I doing the right thing, God? Am I on the right track? Will I ever be of any use to you? Shall I chuck the whole thing and try something else?"

Distinctly he heard the answer come to him across the night: "I can use you. I need you. You make the choice; I will find the way."

Stirred, Billy said: "All right, Lord, if you want me you've got me!"

Now Billy applied himself to his studies with even greater diligence. Dean John R. Minder perceived Billy's dedication and gave him special attention. They became good friends and occasionally took evening walks to discuss studies and the ministry. Billy revealed his special interest in preaching and Dean Minder gave him important advice: know your subject, believe your message, speak it with conviction. In many ways, this was probably the most important lesson Billy learned at the Institute.

So close did Dean Minder and Billy become that one evening Billy told him the story of his shattered romance. The Dean understood.

"You're young, Bill," he said. "There will be many more disappointments ahead for you. You did the right thing in turning completely to God after this episode. The closer you stay to Him the easier the future disappointments will be to endure. When you get home tonight, read Second Corinthians."

Bill did, and in the first chapter he found the words Minder had hinted at, words he held close the rest of his life: "Blessed be the Father of mercies and the God of all comfort, who comforts us in our affliction that we may be able to comfort them that are in any affliction through the comfort wherewith we ourselves are comforted."

On another occasion, Dean Minder asked: "Bill, where do you disappear to so many afternoons? I haven't been able to find you several times when I wanted to see you."

"Oh," Billy said evasively, "I just go for walks."

"Well, walking's healthy," said Minder. "You just walk?"

Billy was embarrassed to tell the truth but he knew he must. "Not always. Sometimes I preach."

"You do? To whom?"

Billy forced a light laugh. "To myself, mostly. And a few animals."

Minder was amused, intrigued. "Really? What is all this?" Billy explained. Minder said: "After all that practice, you must be pretty good. We'll have to find you a real pulpit one of these days."

Billy laughed again, relieved that Minder had not made more out of his woodland habits.

A few days later, on a Sunday, Dean Minder said to Billy: "I'm driving over to Palatka this evening to assist at a service. Care to come along?"

"Very much," said Billy.

When they reached the church the Baptist minister greeted Minder warmly. "I'm so glad you could come," he said. "Would you do us the favor of preaching tonight?"

Minder shook his head. "Not me. Billy Graham is preaching here tonight."

Stung, Billy backed away. "Oh, no, Dean."

"Why not? You've certainly had enough practice."

"But you don't understand. I've never really preached in my life."

"It's time you did. Do you have anything ready?"

"I have four sermons from class," Billy said, "but the four together wouldn't take more than ten minutes."

"Well, you start," Minder said, "and if you run short I'll fill for you."

There was no way out of it. Billy sat nervously on the platform as the Baptist minister performed the preliminary ceremonies. His mind on what he would say, Billy was deaf to what was going on around him, and when he heard his name announced he jumped to his feet as if he had been kicked. Dazed with fear, he approached the lectern as if it were a guillotine. Despite his fear, he presented a handsome picture of a good-looking young man whose finely chiseled features were deep in thought and the congregation gazed up at him expectantly, unaware that they were about to witness a painful baptism in homiletics.

Billy announced his Scripture text, then expounded on it briefly. From this he moved on to the story of his own conversion at Mordecai Ham's meeting and he told how the event had changed his life. He then explained what making the same decision for Christ could do to the lives of others. As he spoke he was aware of a tremor in his voice, which he tried to overcome by speaking louder than necessary. To overcome his shaking knees, he walked back and forth on the platform. To hide his trembling fingers, he either raised his fists to emphasize an idea or he pointed dramatically at anyone whose eyes met his. He wanted desperately to look at his watch to see how long he had been speaking but he could not think of any gesture that would allow it until it occurred to him to throw both arms up over his head. The sudden movement drew back his coat-cuffs and he saw his watch. He had been speaking about fifteen minutes. And he knew he had nothing more to say.

He did the only thing he could. "Now, brother and sisters, you have sat there listening to me speak about Christ," he said. "Now it is your turn to speak for Him. Come forward to the platform. Come forward and declare yourself for Christ. That's the way you can speak for Him in your lives. Come forward, come forward."

To his astonishment, three or four people got up and proceeded down the aisle to him.

Inspired, he went on "Come forward, my friends, come forward to Jesus. If you want some help on this difficult road, raise your hands and I will come down and help you."

A hand went up. It was a man who, from his clothes and appearance, was obviously a woodsman with the physical strength not only to walk down the aisle but to carry a couple of pews with him. Billy stepped down from the platform and went to the man. As he reached out to take the woodsman by the hand, the man said in a loud voice: "You don't need to think because you go to that school down there that you know everything!"

The critical words hit Billy like an uppercut. He stared at the man for a moment, then went back to the platform and turned the service over to the Baptist minister. He suffered until the meeting ended and he was once again in the dark protection of Dean Minder's car.

They drove several silent miles, then Minder said: "Not bad, not bad at all. A little short, but not bad."

"It was awful," Billy said, refusing to be comforted.

"Because somebody took a swipe at you?"

"He was right. I was too smart-alecky."

"For a minute there you did look a little proud of yourself," Minder observed quietly. "Who knows? Maybe God stirred that man to say what he did to take the pride out of you."

"I wasn't proud; I was scared stiff," Billy admitted. "It wasn't until those people started to come forward that I thought I might be pulling it off."

"Preachers don't bring people forward to make their decisions; God does."

Billy accepted the fact in silence.

Dean Minder commented after a moment. "We'll have to find a few more pulpits where you can try your wings."

Billy groaned his dismay.

iii

Billy was troubled for days by the memory of the woodsman. That he might have given an immature and poorly prepared sermon did not bother him; time and experience would give him stature. He was worried, however, that the flash of confidence he felt when the first people came forward might actually have been pride. He knew that pride was wrong in anyone and that in a preacher it could be fatal to his purposes. If, then, he had experienced pride he wanted to beware of it in the future. Caution made him self-conscious; self-consciousness made him uncertain; uncertainty drew him into himself, and he brooded.

Wisely, Dean Minder refused to discuss the subject with

him. The day Billy went to him for guidance Dean Minder avoided the subject by greeting him with: "Bill, I was just going to send for you. The preacher at the United Brethren church in town telephoned me this morning. He's going away this Sunday and wants someone to fill in for him. I suggested you."

"I don't think I should," Billy said, "especially after my last debacle."

Minder pretended innocence. "What in the world are you talking about? I thought you did rather well."

Billy shook his head. "I don't think I'm ready yet, Dean."

"That's not for you to decide," said the Dean. "Now, you know where the church is; the service is at eleven o'clock. Be there."

The next Sunday morning Billy went to the church with the utmost trepidation. The deacons were awaiting him and welcomed him warmly. He looked for hints of their reaction to his youth but saw none. At eleven o'clock he ascended the platform and looked out at the small congregation. Alert and polite faces looked back at him. He began. He led the hymns, he read the church-social announcements, he gave the sermon on which he had worked for three days. It took thirty-five minutes; he felt that if it weren't good enough it was at least long enough. Then he led a final hymn and said a final prayer and left the platform.

Quickly one of the deacons went around to him in the backroom. "Very fine, young man," he said. "We enjoyed your message very much. You come back and see us again, hear?" He offered Billy a plain white envelope.

Billy accepted the envelope absently, relieved by the kind words. "Thank you for having me," he said. "I'll be happy to come back anytime."

Some members of the congregation were still in front of the church when Billy left. He paused to chat with them. One family invited him home for lunch but Billy said he had to get back to the school. It was not until he had returned to the dormitory that Billy remembered he had been handed an envelope. He opened it. It contained $2.25. He was appalled. They had paid him? For what? For preaching the Gospel? But why? He could not take money for that!

He went to look for Dean Minder, but the Dean was away and would not return until Tuesday. It was Wednesday before Minder had time to see Billy.

Billy blurted out: "Those people *paid* me Sunday."

"How much?" Minder asked.

"Two dollars and twenty-five cents." Billy's tone was incredulous.

Minder was not sure he understood it. "So?"

"Dean, I can't take money for preaching the Gospel. It's not right."

The Dean sank back in his chair, impatient but amused. "Oh, the idealism of youth!" he said. "Billy, how do you think preachers pay their bills? Their congregations give them a salary. Preachers have to earn a living, the same as anybody else."

"But I'm not even a preacher yet," Billy argued.

"You did a preacher's job," said Minder.

"Even so, it just doesn't seem right that—"

Minder interrupted him with a raised hand. Then he reached for the Bible and read from First Corinthians: "Know ye not that they that minister about sacred things eat of the things of the temple and they that wait upon the altar have their portion with the altar? Even so did the Lord ordain that they that proclaim the Gospel should live of the Gospel." He closed the book and looked at Billy. "Do you understand that passage?"

Billy answered reluctantly. "Yes, sir."

"Very well, then. The money is yours."

"All right, sir."

Dean Minder glanced away reflectively. "I just hope they pay their regular preacher better than that. How does the man stay alive?"

Despite himself, Billy had to laugh.

Thereafter Billy did not resist the preaching assignments Dean Minder gave him. He preached regularly at a trailer court in Tampa on Sunday mornings; Sunday evenings he preached at various churches up and down the western Florida coast. On one occasion when Dean Minder was called away for extensive conferences he turned his own church over to Billy—an important assignment that brought Billy what struck him as the phenomenal sum of six dollars a Sunday. Some weeks later Dean Minder was called to preach a two-week revival in northern Florida and he took Billy along as an assistant. By now Billy had developed a preaching style of his own. He spoke rapidly, with stern conviction. He moved freely back and forth on the platform. Better acquainted with the Bible, he quoted it frequently. Well planned sermons progressed tensely to the ultimate invitation to come forward and declare for Christ.

Both Billy and Dean Minder spoke each night. At the end of the first week, Minder said: "Billy, I'm going to leave you on your own for the second week. I think you can handle it; it's clear to me that the people are coming more to hear you than to hear me, anyway. I'll come back for the closing service."

For a moment, Billy felt trapped, but then he recognized another of Minder's efforts to make him stand on his own. Determined to do his best for the sake of Minder's faith in him, Billy went through the week with great success. When the Dean returned from the Institute the following Sunday he found a huge crowd at the church long before the service was scheduled to begin.

"This is wonderful, Billy," he said. "I guess you've found your place in life."

"I hope so," said Billy, "but it's sure been terrifying thinking of something to say every night. Tonight I'm supposed to preach on the Second Coming and my mind has gone blank."

"That's a common occurrence among preachers," said Minder, "as strange as it may seem. Let's see what we can work out." They sat down together, paging through the Bible, and in twenty minutes they plotted a sermon that brought the revival to a stirring conclusion with scores of conversions.

People began to talk about the student at the Institute who was such an outstanding speaker and an increasing number of invitations to preach came to Billy. Soon he was leading entire revivals by himself. Baptists particularly liked him and often telephoned the school for his services. Various Baptists groups were considering calling Billy to take over their pulpits when he finished school. At the end of one Baptist revival the offer was definitely put to him.

"I'd be honored," he said, "but there's only one problem. I'm a Presbyterian."

"Well, that can be repaired easily enough," a man said. "You just have to be baptized by immersion. You've been preaching to Baptists so much you're practically one of us anyway. Why not go the whole way?"

"I'll pray about it and let you know," said Billy.

That evening after the final service dozens of Baptists who had been brought closer to Christ through Billy accompanied him to a country lake and witnessed his baptism by immersion. It was, Billy said, a thrilling experience, and it was another important step in the fulfillment of himself.

In May, 1940, Billy completed his studies at the Institute and earned a bachelor's degree in theology. He was also ordained a minister in the St. John's Baptist Association of Northern Florida. The Institute's yearbook said of him:

"Billy Frank Graham, Charlotte, N. C. Activities: President, Senior Class; Assistant Pastor; Chaplain, Tampa Trailer Court; Volley Ball, Swimming. Personal Aim: Evangelist. Favorite Song: Faith of Our Fathers. Favorite Scripture Verse: Jude 3: 'I exhort you that ye should earnestly contend for the faith which was once delivered unto the saints.'"

It seemed that, at 21, Billy had, as Dean Minder put it, found his place in life: a Baptist preacher in Florida. But there were certain factors at work that would change all that. God had bigger plans for him.

Chapter IV

Inexplicably, Billy began to feel the urge for more education. Qualified though he was to preach the Gospels, he felt he needed a broader personal scope. He loved Florida, he was happy with the people he worked with and for, but nevertheless he detected in himself a gnawing desire to expand. He wrote his father of his desire; Frank Graham replied with his approval. In the autumn of 1940, Billy entered Wheaton College, Wheaton, Illinois.

Founded by Wesleyan Methodists in 1853, Wheaton College was interdenominational. Having started out as a one-story limestone building, it had grown to a magnificent institution covering 35 acres and accommodating over a thousand students by the time Billy Graham entered. The school had produced leaders in all professions and businesses, but it was proudest of the hundreds of young people it had produced for the foreign missions around the world. Its atmosphere was highly spiritual; devotional services were held daily and all students were required to attend church on Sundays; the Christian Council was the school's most respected student organization.

It was the perfect place for Billy to acquire further personal and spiritual maturity. There was some surprise among his friends in Florida and North Carolina when he chose to major in anthropology. He had no explanation for it himself, except that he was interested in the ways man had lived in the past. Because of his studies at the Florida Bible Institute, he was permitted to enter Wheaton College in the sophomore year.

A student again, Billy adhered to his policy of earning

his own way. He discovered that Wheaton could use a hauling service, so he rented a truck and made himself available to students, teachers and townfolk who needed a strong young man to move anything from a trunk to a houseful of furniture. Also, he did not arrive friendless at Wheaton. Jimmie Johnson, the young evangelist who had inveigled him into preaching in a North Carolina jail, had entered the college for further studies and the two Tar Heel preachers shared a room on the top floor of a private home.

It was Johnson who circulated the word of Billy's preaching experience in Florida. The students were interested. Billy was asked to speak at one of the morning services. In a short time his reputation spread throughout the Illinois town and he soon found himself with more preaching engagements than he had time to fill. A small gratuity went along with each engagement. By the end of Billy's first year at Wheaton he was earning as much from his speaking as he did from his trucking business. He decided that if he proved to be as busy with preaching the following year he would give up the hauling service. This turned out to be the case, but before he ended his career as a mover he took on one job brought an important influence into his life.

One day the Dean of Women sent him a note: "Please pick up the luggage of Miss Ruth Bell on the five o'clock train from Chicago." As directed, Billy met the train, and he was surprised to meet Ruth Bell herself.

She was a small girl, just five-feet-five, with neat black hair, large brown eyes and attractive features. When Billy found her luggage and saw her standing near it, he asked: "Is this yours?"

"Yes," she said.

"I'm from the college; I'm supposed to haul your luggage to your quarters." He noticed she was carrying a book. He took a closer look at it and saw it was the Bible. He was both surprised and impressed.

She ignored his scrutiny. "Thank you," she said. "Is there a bus or something I can take?"

"You can ride with me," he offered.

She wasn't sure she wanted to. She had a quiet suspicion that the tall, handsome, grinning truck-driver looking down at her was a bit too fresh.

Billy added: "There's plenty of room. And the truck is clean."

She hesitated, then: "All right."

As Billy loaded her trunks he noticed the travel stickers on them, and when he slid behind the wheel he had his conversation-opener ready.

"You've really been around," he said. "I noticed the stickers from China."

She said nothing.

"You been to China?" he went on.

She said yes.

He figured her to be the daughter of millionaires; only millionaires could afford to take trips like that: a Bible-reading millionairess, that was something.

"That must have been a wonderful trip," Billy said. "When were you there?"

"I was born there," Ruth said.

Another surprise. "You don't say!"

"I do."

"How did that happen? I mean, well, it's very unusual."

She gave him a brief look, then turned her face away. "Not really. People are born everyday in China."

Oh. A chilly one. "Americans? You are American, aren't you?"

"My father is a medical missionary," she explained, and she wished he would be quiet.

"That's very interesting," he said, "and important." Out of his own interest in her he lost his concern for careful driving. They careened through the tree-lined Wheaton streets. On one particularly harrowing turn she frowned at him and he slowed down a bit.

He said: "So you've come all the way from China to go to Wheaton College."

"Yes."

"Why Wheaton?"

Would he never shut up so he could pay attention to his driving? "My sister is here."

"Really?"

"Really."

"What's her name?"

"Rosa."

"Rosa Bell? I know her."

She glanced at him again, wondering how her sister had come to know a truck-driver. "You do?"

"Not personally, but I know who she is."

They stopped in front of the house where Rosa and Ruth were to share rooms. Before Billy could help Ruth from the truck, she got out by herself and began to walk to the house. Rosa, watching at a window, saw the truck pull up and hurried down three flights of stairs to meet Ruth. Overjoyed to see each other, the two sisters embraced and kissed and immediately plunged into chatter of news about their parents. Wholly ignored but understanding why, Billy made two trips to the top of the house with Ruth's luggage. He finished the job and met the girls on his last trip down the stairs.

"Well, that's it," he said.

Ruth reached for her purse. "How much do I owe you?"

"Not a thing," said Billy. "Welcome to Wheaton College."

She disapproved. "Thank you," she said, "but I'd rather pay."

"Out of the question," Billy said. "I'll see you around." And he left.

In the same moment he left Ruth's mind. There was too much to discuss with Rosa to talk about a fresh truck-driver. All that evening, the two sisters talked about China and their family, and in the morning Ruth was busy arranging her classes. Billy was completely forgotten.

Actually, Ruth saw Billy again before he saw her. In his second year at Wheaton—his junior year—Billy was appointed pastor of the Wheaton Student Church, an important assignment usually held by older and more experienced men and an appointment that clearly showed the high regard the faculty had for him. On her first

Sunday at Wheaton, Ruth Bell attended services at the church with Rosa. She had just settled in her place and was listening to the last notes of the choir's first selection when she saw Billy enter from the sacristy room and approach the rostrum.

"Rosa, look," she whispered, amazed.

Rosa thought Ruth was reacting to Billy's good looks. "Ruth, please, you're in church."

"It's the truck-driver," Ruth declared.

Rosa corrected her. "It's Billy Graham, one of the students. He drives the truck to earn his tuition."

"But I thought—" The words caught in her throat.

Billy was at the rostrum, waiting for the choir to finish. He let his gaze move over the students seated in front of him. His eyes fell upon Ruth. He permitted a half-smile to come upon his face and he sent her a scarcely perceptible nod of greeting. She lowered her head and wished she were back in China.

ii

Like new friends who quickly discover much in each other to like, Billy and Ruth were intensely interested in each other. She told him how her parents—Dr. and Mrs. L. Nelson Bell—had gone to China in 1916 to work as missionaries at Tsing Kiang Pu, in Kiangsu Province 300 miles north of Shanghai. Doctor Bell was a surgeon and had directed the construction and management of a 380-bed hospital at the Presbyterian mission station. Ruth had been born there in 1920; she could speak Chinese before she learned English. She received her preliminary education at the mission, then had gone on to Korea for higher training, and now she had come to Wheaton. She was majoring in theology. She loved China, she wanted to devote her life to the country, and she expected to return there someday as a missionary. When that would be she did not know. War between China and Japan had wrought many hardships among the missionaries; her parents expected to have to leave China soon for their own safety. But someday she would go back; she was sure of it.

Billy answered her many questions about himself. He told her about the farm at Charlotte, his love of sports and books, his experiences as a Fuller Brush man, his training at Bob Jones College and Florida Bible Institute. The summer he finished at the Institute he related, he had received many invitations to preach at revivals and had accepted one at York, Pennsylvania, that had been rather successful. Because of his age and his youthful appearance, he had been billed as "The Boy Preacher" —a label he disliked but could not escape. Following York, there had been other calls to preach, enough to occupy him fulltime. But he discussed the situation with his parents and decided to go ahead with his plans to attend Wheaton College. If he had decided otherwise, he might never have met Ruth; he trembled at the thought.

They were in love. They both knew it. And they were unhappy about it. Ruth believed that if she married Billy she would have to put aside her desires to be a missionary to China, a desire that was too important to her to dismiss easily. Billy was still sensitive about his dismal adventure at romance with the girl at the Florida school and still winced at the memory of it. Furthermore, he remained determined that no girl, no friend, nothing whatsoever, would detour him from his complete surrender to Christ as an evangelist.

But they were in love. And they didn't know what to do about it.

Ruth said to Rosa: "I don't think Christ led me through twenty years of Chinese diseases and Chinese wars if He didn't intend for me to keep my promise to go back to China as a missionary."

Rosa said: "Don't you think it's possible that Christ led you through twenty years of Chinese diseases and Chinese wars so you could come to Wheaton to meet Billy and marry him?"

Billy said to Jimmie Johnson: "I'm convinced that Jesus means for me to bring souls to Him and I can't do that traipsing all over China."

Jimmie said: "Why not? The Chinese have souls too, you know. How can you be so sure where God wants you to do your preaching?"

Ruth said to Billy: "We can't go on like this; we're seeing too much of each other. But I don't know whether I want to go on with you like this or whether I should start dating other boys."

Billy said: "I don't want you to date other fellows, but I know why you feel you should."

"I need time to think," Ruth said.

"We both do. Let's give ourselves some time."

During this time, Ruth's parents came home from China and settled at Montreat, North Carolina, the site of an important Presbyterian mission training center. Happy to be among old friends, Doctor Bell began a medical practice in nearby Asheville that was soon thriving. Eager to see their daughters at Wheaton, the Bells went north to the school. They met Billy. Although the young couple still were not sure of themselves, Doctor Bell had no doubts about their future. On returning to Montreat, he observed to his wife: "We'll have to keep an eye on that Graham boy. Looks like the Presbyterians are about to lose out to the Baptists again."

Billy and Ruth did not let their uncertainty dim the fun of their friendship. The time they gave themselves they spent together, dating exclusively. Most often the dates were preaching assignments Billy received. Invariably on the way home they discussed the ceremony. One night Ruth decided to tease Billy.

"If you want the truth," she said when he asked her opinion, "I thought you were rather hammy tonight."

He looked at her as if she had struck him. "I was? Gosh."

"Maybe I'm not used to so much histrionics with sermons, but, really, Bill, sometimes you do carry on."

He was mortified. "I had no idea. I'll have to watch myself."

"And you talk so fast, tonight especially. I wonder if the people got everything you said."

He stared glumly at the road ahead. "That's awful. If

people can't understand me, what good can I expect to do?"

"Well," she tried to say lightly, "you asked for my opinion."

"Yes, I did. Thanks for being so honest. I guess I've got a lot of habits that need changing."

She could not carry it on any longer. "Change one and I'll never speak to you again."

Bewildered, he looked at her again and caught her quietly laughing at him. He let his chagrin broaden into a smile. "You've been in China too long," he said. "You've developed a typically inscrutable Chinese personality. I never know where I stand with you."

She was becoming increasingly sure of where he stood. Aware of the decision she would have to make soon, she spent a lot of time in prayer and meditation over it, convinced that if in the end she felt God still wanted her to be a missionary she would be ready to make the sacrifice of the man she loved. Billy made no effort to influence her in either direction, a fact which both puzzled and annoyed her.

She admitted to Rosa: "Sometimes he's so polite, so formal. He rarely treats me as I thought a man treated the woman he loved."

"Maybe he's being cautious," Rosa said. "Being too affectionate could cause all sorts of problems."

Meanwhile, Jimmie Johnson was advising Billy: "Sure you ought to kiss her once in a while, Bill. It's only normal, especially since you both know you're in love. You shouldn't go wild, of course, but a girl expects a little affection once in a while."

Billy was distressed. "I'd like a little affection once in a while myself," he said, "but I don't want to give Ruth the impression that I'm just another campus Romeo."

Ruth's impression of Billy was steadily crystallizing. In her prayers and through her Bible reading, she grew increasingly aware that her place was with him but she said nothing specific to him. The weeks passed and the end of the school year approached. On one of their last dates before summer vacation Billy got on the subject of missionary work.

Ruth said: "I'm beginning to think my missionary work will be confined to our children."

Her oblique remark escaped Billy at first, then he interrupted his next sentence to ask: "What did you say about our children?"

"You heard me," Ruth said.

"Then you will marry me?"

"I think it would be my greatest joy."

He wanted to get one point clear. "It won't be an easy life, you know, married to a wandering evangelist. We'll be separated a great deal."

"I don't think being apart necessarily means being separated," Ruth said.

He kissed her.

They decided to wait until after their graduation to be married. During their last year at Wheaton College, Billy's reputation as a preacher spread throughout Northern Illinois. Before the year was out, he was offered the pastorate of the First Baptist Church in Western Springs, outside Chicago. Billy knew the offer meant a detour from the distinct evangelism he preferred, but he decided to accept it for several important reasons. World War II was then in progress; Billy had thought of becoming a chaplain, but he knew there was a shortage of pastors in the country, just as there was a shortage of medical doctors, and in the same attitude that many doctors felt their place was at home attending civilians so Billy felt that the ministry at home should not be neglected. Also, he was aware that he was in personal need of some practical experience in the business of church work—the headaches of the financial aspects of church affairs. Furthermore, he realized that eventually he would be traveling greatly and he wanted to have at least a few months of quiet married life with Ruth.

They were graduated in June; they set their marriage for August 13, 1943. A friend of Ruth's consulted a calendar and exclaimed: "That's a Friday! What fool is going to get married on Friday, the thirteenth?"

"I am," Ruth said calmly.

They were married at Montreat. Ruth made her own wedding gown, as she made most of her own clothes. The gown was heavy with laces and veils and a long trail. Ruth was afraid she would wrinkle it on the drive to the church, and to prevent damage she stood up in the rear of the car, bending over the front seat in an awkward position unbecoming a bride-to-be but effective in the protection of her dress.

They spent their honeymoon at a tourists' inn at Blowing Rock, North Carolina—seven days for $70, which was all that Billy could afford. His assignment at Western Springs was to pay him $45 a week, but that would not start until September; meanwhile Billy was occupied with southern revivals for which he was not paid. The marriage, at least in terms of money, was off to a poor start. One Sunday when they attended church together Billy thought he was putting a one-dollar bill into the collection plate, only to discover too late that it was a ten-dollar bill.

"We'll have to cut down on other things for a while," he told Ruth. "But at least the money went to a good cause."

"Keep one thing in mind," Ruth said, teasing. "You won't get any credit in the eyes of the Lord for giving the ten dollars because, after all, you only intended to give one."

Billy threw up his arms in mock disgust. "That's what I get for marrying a theologian!" he cried.

iii

In September they were in Western Springs. The First Baptist Church was not actually a church. It was a basement; the church had yet to be built. Also, there was no parsonage and practically no congregation. At his first service, Billy addressed 35 people. But he was young and hard-working, and he decided that all the congregation needed was a shot in the arm. He provided it by quickly embarking on a wide range of church projects.

He appointed a building committee to work for the construction of the church itself; he devised a pay-as-you-go program by which donation pledges could be fulfilled over a long period, thereby easing the financial burden on the members of the congregation. He organized a mission circle, with Ruth as its advisor. The interest in the missions put new life into the congregation. Liking children, Billy was anxious to work with them; in a short time the church had the busiest youth program in town. Most pastors would have been satisfied if the majority of such a small congregation attended church with some regularity on Sunday mornings; Bill was not. He inaugurated Sunday evening services which he conducted on an evangelistic basis, attracting people from other churches where no Sunday evening ceremonies were held. Billy also became a popular speaker at luncheon clubs and through them met men who were willing to help his building program; by spring the building committee was ready to start studying blueprints for a church to be erected as soon as the war allowed. An extremely active man, Billy realized he still could become an Army chaplain, serving a camp near Chicago while continuing as a pastor without pay. He proposed the idea to the Army and it was approved. Thus in a matter of a few months, Billy was becoming a very popular young man with a growing following.

Among the following was Torrey Johnson, an older man who had already established himself as a prominent Chicago clergyman. He was the founder of the Midwest Bible Church, a popular evangelistic congregation; he had a weekly radio program; he taught Greek at the Northern Baptist Seminary; he was the organizer of a new movement called Youth for Christ, which was then restricting itself to rallies among servicemen at their training camps. Johnson had first heard about Billy while he was still at Wheaton College and went there to hear him speak. When Billy settled at Western Springs, Johnson was one of the first Chicago-area ministers to befriend him, bringing him actively into Baptist circles and invited Billy and Ruth to dinner often to meet other church leaders.

At one such dinner, Johnson asked: "What are your plans, Bill? You're young; you have the world before you. Is there anything special you have in mind?"

"I want to do whatever the Lord wants me to do," Billy said simply. "I expect He'll let me know what that is as time goes on. Meanwhile, the Army is ready to accept me as a chaplain in this area and I should be called up any day now. When the world settles down I'd like to go to theological school; there is so much more I've got to learn. Then evangelism, of course."

Johnson considered it. "Theological school? I wonder about that, Bill. I've heard you preach and it seems to me you've already got plenty to say. The pulpit—that's where you belong. Stay there and preach; that's what I'd advise."

Billy shrugged; he did not want to make an issue of the matter at a dinner table. He tried to make a joke out of it. "I ought to learn some theology. I'm married to a woman with a degree in theology and I ought to be able to hold my own with her to assert my masculine superiority. The only trouble is that she's a Presbyterian theologian."

Johnson was surprised and amused. "Presbyterian, are you?"

Ruth smiled and nodded, wondering where the conversation would go.

Billy said: "Before I had a church of my own, we used to alternate, going to a Baptist church one Sunday and a Presbyterian church the next, just to keep peace. I haven't got any money, but I'll pay a hundred dollars to the person who can convince Ruth to be baptized by immersion."

Johnson looked at Ruth with open affection. "I don't think you'll ever have to pay out the hundred, Bill. But then a fiery Baptist needs a cool-minded Presbyterian on his team. There shouldn't be too much trouble in your house." He was right on both counts: Ruth remained a

Presbyterian and there was no trouble in the house over it.

One afternoon near Christmas, Torrey Johnson telephoned Billy and said: "My doctor tells me I've been working too hard and have to cut down."

"I'm sorry to hear that," Billy said. "Is it serious?"

"No, just exhaustion, I suppose. I'm getting to be an old man, I guess."

"Not that old," Billy said, then asked: "Is there anything I can do for you, Torrey?"

"Yes, there is. I have this Sunday night radio program, you know."

"I listen to it every week," Billy said.

"I'd like you to do more than that," said Johnson. "I'd like you to take it over, you and your church."

"Me?"

"Yes, you."

"Gosh, Torrey," Billy said, "that's an important job. Shouldn't it go to a more experienced man, somebody who's better known in Chicago?"

"I'm asking you to do it," Johnson insisted.

Billy didn't know what to say. "I'm not sure I can decide this by myself," he observed. "There's too much involved. What does the program cost, Torrey?"

"The radio time is $150 a week."

"That's more than we get in our Sunday collections," Billy admitted. "I don't think my people can afford it. We've got a building-fund campaign going and the youth program costs and—"

Johnson interrupted. "Don't decide now. Talk it over with Ruth and with your deacons and pray about it. I'll call you back on Monday."

On Sunday morning, Billy put the proposition plainly to his congregation, now numbering 70 from about 25 families. He told them the positive aspects first—the opportunity for all of them to share in spreading the Gospels, of bringing spiritual comfort to shut-ins, of catching the attention of the casual dial-twister who stood in need of salvation.

"But," he said, "the simple fact is that we can't afford

it. Our average Sunday collection is $125, which we need to run the church. The radio time costs $150. If we're going ahead with it we must first find someway to pay for it. Does anybody have any ideas?"

A man raised his hand. "Will you be able to ask for donations on the air?"

"Yes, but indirectly, and then hope for the best," Billy said. "But I don't think the station will sell us the time on the hopes of being paid."

Another man stood up. "What do you think of the idea of us donating money to pay for the show for a while until we see what the mail response is?"

"Is it possible?" Billy returned.

"I'm willing to give ten dollars a week, if that will help."

"It sure will."

Another man said: "I can give ten dollars a week for a while."

A woman said: "We can give five."

Through such personal sacrifices, the congregation was able to pledge $85 a week, but it was not enough.

Billy said: "I don't think we ought to miss the chance to do this work for the Lord. Let's sign the contract and trust to Him."

The program was called Songs In The Night and was broadcast on Sunday evening on station WENR from ten-thirty to eleven-fifteen from the church. Its emphasis was on Gospel singing; in the week Billy had to prepare for the first broadcast he managed to muster a passable choir from the Western Springs churches. Between songs there were prayers and Bible-reading and short, evangelistical talks by Billy. The broadcast was made from the church itself. Despite the fact that the engineer was the only professional present, the first program went off surprisingly well. Billy closed the broadcast with a subtle appeal for donations, saying that the program could only continue on the generosity of the listeners.

All day Monday he worried how the program had been received. Torrey Johnson telephoned him congratulations; so did a few other ministers, but that was all. On Tuesday, the first mail arrived—a half dozen letters of praise and gratitude, but no money. On Wednesday, the bill arrived from the station.

But in the same mail were over fifty letters from listeners, most of them containing donations—enough at least to make up the difference between $85 and $150. Thursday's mail was equally rewarding; Friday's dropped off but it was still encouraging. Billy could go on the air the following Sunday with the confidence that not only did he have listeners, but generous listeners indeed.

Billy tried something unusual. As an evangelist, he was deeply concerned about individual decisions for Christ. In a church or a tent, he could lead a normal sermon around to the call for such decisions effectively, but on the radio program his intermittent talks were seldom five minutes long—scarcely enough time to put proper emphasis on the important personal act. Nevertheless, he felt he must try: it was, he felt, his duty to try. He tried, putting his whole heart and soul into his final sermonette, pleading with his listeners to make their own decisions for Christ in their homes and to let him know by mail if they did so. His pleas were so direct, so piercing, so spiritually penetrating, that they earned response. The letters came. People in their homes, separated from Billy by miles and yet touched by the vitality of his call, were accepting Christ as their savior and vowing to live by His precepts. Thus the program became not only an opportunity for Billy but a privilege.

There came, too, numerous invitations for Billy to preach to churches and clubs, as many as twenty a day. He could not possibly accept them all, but he took as many as he could, eager to meet the people who were now supporting the weekly broadcast comfortably beyond its cost. To improve the program, Billy used some of the surplus to hire a professional singer to perform the beloved Gospel songs. He was George Beverly Shea, then an announcer and singer on Radio Station WBMI, operated by the Moody Bible Institute. It was the beginning of a lifelong friendship and association.

For almost a year, Billy kept up the rugged pace of

running his church, making the broadcasts and speaking to the groups that called on him. During the summer of 1944, when most churches slowed down their activities, he was as busy as ever. The toll for such extravagant energy struck in the fall. Billy suffered an attack of the mumps that sent him to bed for weeks. Despite every effort, he could not shake the prolonged after-effects of the disease. He was forced to give up all his work. The Army informed him that the demand for chaplains had decreased and that, in view of his long illness, he was being removed from military lists.

Ruth's father wrote that perhaps the bitter cold Illinois winter was a factor in Billy's long recuperation and he suggested that if it was at all possible Billy and Ruth should go to Florida. Their lean bank account scarcely provided for such luxury, but they admitted that Doctor Bell was probably right. It was better to spend the money and hope that the sun would cure Billy than to approach the busy Christmas season without sufficient strength for all the work that would have to be done.

So they went to Florida. They had just checked into their hotel when the telephone rang. Billy answered it. He heard:

"Is that you, Bill? This is Torrey Johnson. I say, this is amazing."

"What's amazing?" Billy asked.

"I just phoned Western Springs to talk to you and they told me you were here."

"I'm in the same hotel with you!" Johnson exclaimed. "Talk about the Hand of God!"

"What do you mean?"

"Bill, I want to talk to you right away. Can I come down to your room?"

"Of course, Torrey, but we're just unpacking," Billy said. "Can you wait until lunch—or is what you've got to say as important as you make it sound?"

"It may be the most important thing in your life," Torrey said.

It turned out to be precisely that.

Chapter V

Looking back on it, Billy Graham never doubted the influence of God in the coincidence that he and Torrey Johnson should choose to stay at the same Florida hotel. Had this not happened, had Johnson not been able to locate Billy at the crucial moment, the lives of millions might well have evolved quite differently because the life of Billy Graham would have been different.

Johnson was at Billy's door before Billy and Ruth could adjust to the surprise of finding him so near. "What a blessing that you didn't go to another hotel," Johnson said as he came in. "A decision has to be made today, and if I hadn't been able to locate you we could all be worse off."

"What in the world is going on?" Billy asked.

"Youth For Christ," Johnson said. "We're going ahead on a greatly expanded program and we want you in it."

"You'd better start at the beginning," Billy suggested.

"Well, you know the program," Johnson said to begin.

"Of course. I've attended some of the rallies."

"But those were at military installations only," Johnson pointed out. "Now we're expanding the movement on an international basis. We've seen what fine work can be done on limited grounds; now we're ready for something big."

Fine work had indeed been done. The original idea behind the Youth For Christ movement had been to provide servicemen with something to do on Saturday nights. Johnson, in organizing the program, had realized that the millions of servicemen on duty in Stateside camps inevitably grew bored with their routine existence and that on Saturday nights, their one night off, their efforts to escape boredom could lead them into serious predicaments. Johnson's plan was to occupy the young men on the dangerous nights, and he quite openly gave his program a religious connotation by calling it Youth For Christ. The armed forces welcomed the program, but there were many sceptics who said it would never work. Most men in uniform, the sceptics said, were out to prove their masculinity by carousing as much as they could; you would never get them to attend what amounted to a church service on Saturday night. But the sceptics had misjudged American youth. The men attended the services, and attendance grew steadily over the war years. The program began in the Chicago area, then expanded across the country. In most cases, the programs followed the same pattern: audience-singing of popular songs, vaudeville acts—magicians, tumblers, clean-minded comedians, hymns, a spiritual talk. Occasionally, the program ended with an altar call. The good that was accomplished by the war-time rallies could never be measured this side of Judgment Day, but that good was accomplished could not be denied.

Johnson said to Billy: "If the recent war news is any yardstick, peace should come soon. When that happens, all the youngsters we've been reaching in military camps will be dumped on the streets of their hometowns and will face moral problems all over again. Now, I've been reading about industry getting ready to convert to peacetime production. I think Youth For Christ has to get ready to convert, too."

"That's certainly practical and reasonable," Billy conceded. "But—"

"This morning," Johnson interrupted, "I had a round-robin telephone conference with my people across the country. We agree that we should start our peace program right now. We should move out of the camps into arenas, ball parks, theatres—anything we can get, and we should appeal not only to young men but girls as well. We want to do this on a big scale, big publicity, big crowds, and we want to turn everyone of our young people into missionaries for Christ among their own friends."

"Fine," Billy said, sincerely, patiently.

"To make this work," Johnson said, "we're going to need the best talent we can find—people the youngsters will know about and want to hear. That's where you come in, Billy."

"Where?"

"We want you to be our first field representative. We want you to go out with a team of men and organize the rallies and be the principal speaker."

Billy did not answer. He got up from his chair and began to pace the room with heavy steps, his eyes downcast. When at last he spoke, he turned to Johnson and said simply: "Gosh, Torrey, I'd love to, but I'm not sure I'm your man."

"We think you are," Johnson said.

"It would mean giving up my pastorate."

"You once admitted to me that you expected to do that someday. You've always wanted evangelism."

"Things have changed." Billy glanced a question at Ruth and she nodded. "Ruth is going to have a baby."

"Wonderful!" said Johnson. "I'm happy for both of you."

Billy accepted the congratulations with a nod. "But you can understand why I don't want to be separated from her too much during this period."

"You won't be. Oh," Johnson said, "you'll be busy enough, rest assured. But these rallies take time to organize. It'll be months before they begin to pile up on you. If you like, we can see to it that you have a month off when Ruth's time comes so you can be with her. I might as well give you the practical side of it, too: you'll be paid $75 a week, plus all expenses when you're on the road. That ought to give you two a better chance to save up a little than you've had at Western Springs."

Billy shrugged off the point. "That's not important."

"What is important is whether or not you'll accept the invitation." Johnson's tone was firm.

"I'll have to think about it," Billy said.

"There isn't much time. I've got to know right away, in case we have to find someone else."

Billy looked at Ruth again. She said: "Take it, Bill. It's what you've always wanted."

"It's what I've always felt God wanted me to do," Billy said. "But the baby—"

"Good heavens, Bill," Ruth said, "I want to have lots of babies, but I don't want your work to come to a standstill every time I'm pregnant. You told me once that your work might often take you away. Well, now it starts. All right. We'll manage. I certainly don't have to tell you that your work means as much to me as it does to you, darling."

Billy thought about it for a moment, then said: "Okay, Torrey, Okay."

ii

They remained in Florida a few weeks to give Billy time to recuperate from his illness, then returned to Western Springs. Billy resigned his pastorate and withdrew from the radio program. However, the impetus he had provided to the Western Springs church lived on. Where once there had been only a basement chapel a magnificent church arose, where once only 35 people worshipped the congregation grew to over a thousand, where once Billy started a mission circle a group developed that supported a score of foreign missionaries, and for many years the Sunday night radio program continued to provide consolation and inspiration to millions of listeners.

Despite the excitement his new life offered, Billy left Western Springs reluctantly. In his sixteen months there he had met good people who were to become lifelong friends and he had witnessed first-hand the willingness in Christians to work hard and sacrifice for God and the church they loved. He was never to have a church of his own again, but his experience at Western Springs gave him a deep and lasting affection for all churches and the people who filled them.

It was in January, 1945, that Billy Graham and Torrey Johnson entered for the first time the two-room office suite they had rented in a downtown Chicago building for the Youth For Christ headquarters. There was no furniture, no telephone, the electricity had not been turned on. And yet both men realized the importance of what they were starting and the empty rooms seemed luxurious to them. Without having to discuss it, they closed the door behind them and knelt down to pray. Together, they offered themselves, their work and American youth to Christ, declaring that any success would be His, not theirs, and that only if He were willing to use them as His tools could they achieve anything at all.

The next weeks were frantic with work. They bought funiture, they put in a phone, they ordered stationery, they wrote publicity releases, they called on ministers throughout the city to get their support for a rally to be held early that spring at Orchestra Hall. At the same time they corresponded with clergymen across the country, arranging rallies for the rest of the year. Trusting so fervently in God, they did not even consider that the first civilian rally might fail, but they wondered to what extent they might succeed because they knew the future of the entire movement depended on the outcome of their first effort.

Ruth Graham soon got used to seeing Billy only at odd hours, when he rushed into the apartment for a clean shirt or a quick meal or a few hours' rest. She shared his enthusiasm for the project and joined his prayers for its success. A practical woman at the same time, however, she felt there was another matter to settle.

"Bill," she said one evening, "let's decide now where we'll call home."

"Chicago, I guess," Bill said. "This is headquarters."

"Yes," she agreed, "while you're here, but you know perfectly well that soon you'll be traveling constantly and headquarters will be wherever you are."

He looked across the table at her, all love and expectation, aware that she had already made up her mind. "What do you suggest, dear?"

"Well," she began, "we're living in furnished apartments, we don't own a stick of furniture, we really have no roots. I've been thinking we ought to choose a place as our own headquarters, some place quiet and beautiful where you can come and rest between rallies."

"Yes?"

"I was thinking of Montreat."

"Montreat's fine," Billy said. "Your folks are there and my family is nearby at Charlotte. Montreat is the place, all right. We'll have to build a home there someday."

Ruth was amused. "Build? Have you taken a look at our bank account lately?"

He knew she was ready now to get the point and he waited.

"Billy," she said, "in the next few months I don't want to be alone too much, so I think I'll go down to Montreat now and stay with my parents until the baby comes. You're all tied up with the rally and Dad's a doctor and—"

He nodded. He hated the thought of being separated, but he realized Ruth was right. "Yes, I suppose it is the best place for you right now."

"And I think we ought to rent a house for a while before we build one," she went on. "The missionaries in Montreat are always coming and going: I can watch for a house for us and have it all ready when you can come down."

"When will you be going?"

"In the next few days."

"All right. It's best, I guess. I'll miss you. I'll write you everyday. And phone you. I'll have Torrey arrange my schedule so I can be in Montreat when it's time for the baby to come."

She could see how sad he was and her heart was touched. She reached across the table and took his hand. "There's somebody I want to meet someday," she said.

"Who?"

"That girl in Florida who turned you down."

"Really? Why?"

"I want to thank her. If she had accepted you, I wouldn't be here with you now."

"Silly," Billy said gently, and he leaned across and kissed Ruth.

Thus a new phase began in the lives of Ruth and Billy Graham, one that would last their whole lives. With the world for his pulpit, Billy would be traveling most of the time and Ruth would be at Montreat. Few married couples, especially of such prominence, would have to rely so much on the mails, on telephones and telegrams, to exchange their daily love. There would at times be months of separation, thousands of miles between them, but as Ruth had once put it they were not actually apart. Rarely, outside of wars, perhaps, had love been put to such tests, but rarely had there been such a couple as this, a couple whose love for each other encompassed a love of God, to whose service they were both dedicated.

Billy's first letters to Montreat blazed with plans for the Orchestra Hall rally. The Chicago ministry was thoroughly cooperative; the hall would surely be packed with youngsters. The newspapers gave the rally a great deal of publicity; the Hearst papers particularly supported the movement, and there was talk that William Randolph Hearst himself was interested in the work. Billy was happy when George Beverly Shea, the professional singer he hired for Western Springs, agreed to take part in the Orchestra Hall program and, if things went well, to go on the road to other rallies. "Everything points to a highly successful night," Billy wrote Ruth.

But when the night came Billy was terrified. Three thousand Chicago teenagers filled the hall, accompanied by some of their ministers, men of outstanding calibre and reputation. It was the biggest crowd Billy had addressed. As he waited in the wings, he suffered pangs of doubt. His uncertainty made him remember his days in Florida when, to develop confidence, he had gone out to the woods and preached to himself. If there had been any woods near Orchestra Hall, Billy would have darted into them, he was sure.

He was, plainly, the main event. The program led up to his talk. Because of his radio program, he was already known to most of his audience. Instead of consoling him, this imbued him with a deep sense of responsibility. He wanted to be sure that he would say the right things. His audience was young, and yet he spoke to them with mature respect.

"This is the finest period of your lives," he said. "Few of you have been touched by what we might call the cruel facts of life. The ideals and ambitions you have now can make great men and women out of you. But you can't fulfill the promise of yourselves alone. You need Christ. You need Him right now, every moment of your daily life. Without Him, you are in trouble. With Him, there can be no trouble too great for you to conquer. But you have to decide whether you will be with Him or without Him. The Bible says: 'He who is not with me is against me.' Where do you stand? Do you want to be with Christ? The Bible says, 'Ask and thou shalt receive.' Have you asked? Do you want to ask? You can, you know, you can ask tonight, right here. You can ask, and God will give you the faith to believe in Him implicitly, He will give you the strength to survive any temptation. But you've got to give Him something, too: you've got to give Him yourself. And you've got to show Him that you are giving yourself to Him, show Him and everybody else. You've got to declare yourself for Him. You've got to decide for Him. Once you've decided, you've got to have the courage to declare yourselves openly. I want you to decide now. And then I want you to have the courage of your convictions by declaring yourself openly by coming forward to the stage, where some of our people will be waiting to help you along this new road you have chosen. Decide for Christ now, tonight, right here. I promise you your life will be different and wonderful!"

He reached their hearts. Forty of them came forward to make their decisions. Ministers reported later that

...ndreds more became more active, more vital members of their churches. The rally was undeniably a success, a lasting success. The road was now open to many more.

iii

In his first year with Youth For Christ, Billy Graham traveled over 200,000 miles to rallies in 47 states. Often his audiences numbered as high as 20,000 youngsters; in that year, 7,000 publicly responded to Billy's invitation to make their decisions for Christ. There had not been such a spiritual force in the country for years; there had never been such a force among the young. It occurred at a desperate moment. The war was ending; idle evenings were increasingly available to the young in search of something to do; juvenile delinquency was beginning its rise. To be able to attract an army of young people to what was plainly a religious meeting was an achievement; to convince 7,000 of them to dedicate their lives to Christ was phenomenal. Billy took no personal credit for it, attributing his success to his own decision for Christ and Christ's willingness to use him to attract others.

The summer of that year Billy took time off to rush to Montreat for the birth of his first child, a girl who was named Virginia and immediately nicknamed Gigi. He was stunned with joy when he beheld his daughter for the first time, deeply grateful that God should present him with someone so lovely, so beautiful, and grateful, too, that Ruth was well and as happy as he.

"This is the first," Ruth told him. "I want more, at least five more."

Billy laughed. "At this rate, we can have a youth rally right in the family."

To add to their happiness, Ruth had found a house directly across the street from her parents. It was small, but certainly adequate for the present, it was partially furnished and the price was reasonable. They decided to take it. They had a home at last.

Even at the start, Billy did not have much time for it.

Fortunately, his next rally was at Asheville, just a few miles away, and although Billy was kept away for long hours at a time he was nevertheless able to return to Ruth at night. It was also at Asheville that Billy acquired another friend who was to remain with him for life. The regular song-leader of the rallies failed to arrive at Asheville. Billy was perturbed. The singing was important. Not only did singing help relax the audience, but Billy believed the old adage that he who sings hymns once prays twice. The song-leader had to be a skilled man, with a casual air, a friendliness, a warmth that could make self-conscious people loosen up and sing out. Now the rally was about to begin and there was no song-leader.

Someone said: "Cliff Barrows is out in the hall."

"Who's he?" Billy asked.

"Cliff's done a lot of choir work here in town. He's pretty good."

Billy shook his head. "No amateurs. This work is too important."

"Well, looks like it's Cliff or nobody."

Billy realized that. He was stuck. "Go get him."

Cliff Barrows was surprised to find himself called backstage. He was introduced to Billy, who told him what the problem was. "Do you think you can handle it?" Billy asked.

"I'll try," Barrows offered.

"Be friendly. Help them to unwind."

"Yes, sir. I know many of these people."

"Good. All right, go on out," Billy said. "By the way, do you know Faith Of Our Fathers? That's my favorite."

"Yes, sir. We can do that one for you." And he walked on stage.

Billy listened apprehensively. He heard a scattered applause from people who recognized Barrows. Barrows cleared his throat nervously, then said: "Eve'n, friends. I just want to say that you can't be more surprised to see me up here than I am." There was some laughter. He went on: "It seems the man who usually does the song-leading couldn't make it here to Asheville tonight, and he can't be sorrier about that than I am." More laughter.

Barrows said: "I expect tonight we'll be hearing a bit about forgiveness, so we might as well start out with some right now. If I don't do a good job out here, I know Billy Graham will forgive me and I hope you will." There was a murmur of approval. Then: "Shall we begin with *Faith Of Our Fathers?* That's what I'm relying on right now."

The organ began; an auditorium of throats were cleared; thousands of voices broke into vibrant song. Barrows chose another hymn, then another. The crowd sang with vigor and enthusiasm. Standing in the wings, Billy said: "He's terrific." When Barrows came off, Billy said to him: "Do you need a job?"

"No, sir," said Barrows, "but I'll take this one if you're offering it."

With that began an association that continued over the ensuing years; Cliff Barrows' face, voice and charm became well known and admired by the millions to attend Billy Graham meetings all over the world.

The world proved to be wide indeed. In the next two years, Billy traveled 750,000 miles, which included four revivals in Europe. The very words Youth For Christ became part of everyday language everywhere, and its influence became part of everyday life. Billy's arrival in a city brought out the reporters who wanted to know more about him. Billy refused to talk about himself; he wanted no personal publicity; he talked only about his work, about the program. This at first gave some reporters the impression that Billy was cool and aloof, but when they let him talk about his work they detected a man who was intensely concerned with the spiritual welfare of the young and heatedly determined to improve it. They found a man who paced the floor in deep thought as he answered their questions, who was lucid, direct and uncomplicated, who, for that matter, did not hesitate during their interviews to question the reporters about the condition of their own souls.

There was some opposition, most of it from ministers. Some were opposed because they thought the rallies were too high-spirited. Others said Billy did not give the youngsters any solid theology, merely holy pep-talks. Billy and his team were ridiculed as "Christian gypsies," and as spiritual hucksters who were not stirring religion but merely peddling it. Billy himself was challenged on the grounds of having insufficient educational background in religion for what he was trying to do.

The criticism did not harm the work, but nevertheless it hurt Billy personally. He wanted no argument with the clergy; he was not attempting to draw congregations away from churches. On the contrary, he invariably urged his audiences to take more active part in their own church affairs. Local ministers were always included on the rally committees. Billy made a point of arriving in a city early enough before the rally to meet with the clergy and devise methods of getting the most out of the project. As for his personal capacities, Billy was well aware of his shortcomings. For the rest of his life he would regret not having studied theology. Even so, the scope of his faith included the confidence that the Holy Spirit would provide him with the right things to say when the necessity arose. In an effort to deepen his knowledge, however, Billy read theologians voluminously while traveling and between rallies at Montreat. Also, the fact remained that Bill encompassed all theologies: he offered something to everybody. That was the basis of his broad appeal.

On one of his trips to England, Billy encountered the strongest opposition of his career. The Youth For Christ rally was to be held in Birmingham, in a municipal arena. Advance workers had obtained the necessary permit to use the auditorium and were busy among the local clergy arranging the program and the attendance. Billy arrived in London where he was to spend a few days meeting reporters and preparing his talks.

It seemed that the British reporters had ganged up on Billy. With their typical rejection of anything American, they baited him with loaded questions and wrote about him with tongue-in-cheek. America, they commented, had apparently developed a new export product: religion. They asked: Wouldn't Americans be wiser to keep their religion at home and try to benefit from it themselves—they could use it.

Billy made no effort to retaliate. To do so, he felt, would detract from his purpose in England. He was there to stimulate love for God and he felt he could not do so by engaging in conflict between men. He read the papers, put them aside, then went to work on his sermons.

One afternoon he received a telephone call from Birmingham: the permit to use the city arena had been rescinded.

"Why?" Billy asked.

"We're not sure," the caller said, "but it looks like some of the clergy got to the members of the city council and convinced them that the rally might be a bad idea after all. What do you want us to do?"

"What can you do?" Billy asked.

"Not very much. But at least we can put up a good fight."

"I don't want any fights. Let me think about it for a while. I'll call you back."

Why had it happened? There was no really specific answer. For reasons of their own, enough of the local ministry opposed the rally to influence the council against Billy. Why did they oppose it? Who knew? Birmingham was mostly Church of England—historically—if not entirely theologically—a Protestant church, a sedate church. Perhaps the church leaders simply did not like rallies, at least American-type rallies; certainly they could not object to anything Billy had to say. In any event, with no permit there could be no rally. A great deal of time, money and talent had been wasted. Billy refused to fight. All he could do now was go home.

The telephone rang again; it was the reception clerk. "Doctor Browne is here to see you, sir," the clerk said.

Doctor Browne? Billy was puzzled. "I haven't sent for a doctor," he said.

"He says it's important that he see you."

Perhaps the man wanted to see him on a spiritual matter. "All right," Billy said. "Send him up."

A few minutes later when Billy opened the door he

recognized his caller to be one of England's most famous evangelists. "Doctor Browne!" Billy said, pleased. "I didn't know it was you. Please come in."

"Thank you for seeing me," said Browne. "I know I haven't an appointment, but I felt I had to come here."

"I'm honored," Billy said. They sat down.

Browne said: "I'm sure you're very busy, preparing for the Birmingham rally."

Billy frowned. "I'm afraid there isn't going to be a rally. The Birmingham council has rescinded our permit."

"Whatever for?"

"I'm not sure. I understand some of the Birmingham ministry doesn't like the idea of the rally."

"How dreadful. What are you going to do?"

"I haven't decided yet."

"You absolutely must go to Birmingham and talk to the councilmen and make an issue of this."

Billy shrugged. "I don't want to cause any more controversy than already exists."

Browne sank back in his chair. "I had no idea I would meet you on an occasion like this. I must tell you something. About an hour ago I was working in my study when I was overwhelmed by a tremendous desire to come here and meet you. I can't explain why this urge should strike me when it did and as powerfully as it did. Actually I wasn't thinking about you; my mind was on something else entirely. But suddenly there it was and I knew I had to see you."

"I'm glad you did," said Billy. "I need a friend right now."

"I couldn't have known that," Browne said. "Even so, I don't think I'm here merely to console you. Tell me, do you believe the Holy Spirit sometimes impels us to do certain things?"

"Of course I do."

"That's the point. At the same moment I felt this urge to come here," Browne went on, "I found myself vividly aware that you possess a vital destiny. It was not my own thought, mark you. It was as if someone had said it to me, out loud. Matter of fact, now that I think of it, I remember that I said aloud that I agreed. I believe it was He who spoke to me."

"The Holy Spirit?"

"Yes. And I believe it was He who sent me here to you, to bless you and pray with you."

The two men exchanged an understanding glance and, without speaking, they knelt. It was Browne who prayed, acknowledging the divine inspiration that had taken him to the hotel and asking the Holy Spirit to give guidance to Billy, not only at this desperate hour but throughout his life. Then Browne arose and went to Billy and placed his hands upon Billy's head, beseeching the Holy Spirit to abide in Billy from then on, specifically, actively, lovingly. This, if ever there was one, was a baptism of the Spirit.

The two men were silent a long time, then Browne said: "You and I are now brothers in a unique way. You realize that, don't you?"

"Yes. I'm grateful you were sent to me; I always shall be."

"I'm sure of it. Now," said Browne, "I must go. You have a lot to do, and I know you'll do the right thing in Birmingham."

They shook hands; Browne left. Immediately Billy began to pack. Then he put through a call to Birmingham. "I'm on my way," he said.

There was panic in the Youth For Christ headquarters when Billy entered. A crowd of workers rushed at him, throwing questions, complaints, anger and tears.

Billy held up his hands. "Just a minute, please," he cried. "Let's calm down. We'll never get anything done in the middle of all this chaos. Now, before we do anything else we're going to take time to pray, so will everyone please be quiet for a moment."

Silence came abruptly. Billy said a prayer, putting the whole matter in God's hands.

Then he said: "Does anybody have a list of the city councilmen?" One was given him. "I want to meet these men."

"It won't do any good," someone said.

Billy said: "They changed their minds once; they may change them again."

In the circumstances, this was extremely audacious. It could almost be foolhardy. Having submitted to the pressures of the local ministry, the councilmen could scarcely reverse their position again without infuriating the clergy or making themselves look silly. Billy knew this; he knew, too, how slim his chances were, but he knew, as well, that he would have to try. The experience with Doctor Browne had left him with an apostolic audacity: he would not fight, but he would not stand idly by.

He went to the office of the first councilman on his list. The man was appalled to learn Billy had arrived. Too embarrassed to see him but too dazed to refuse him, the councilman kept Billy waiting half an hour before admitting him into his private room. Then he welcomed Billy coolly, apprehensively.

He said archly: "I suppose you are here about the permit?"

"Yes, sir," Billy said.

"I suppose you want to know why it was revoked?" Billy said: "No, sir."

The man was caught off balance. "You don't?"

"No, sir. I realize you had your reasons for changing your mind, but that is your business. It wouldn't do me any good to know why you did it."

"No, I guess not," the councilman conceded. "Then why are you here?"

"Well, I hope I'll be able to change your mind again," Billy said humbly.

"Not much chance of that," the man said. "A final decision has been made and it stands."

"Will you give me a minute to tell you about our program?" Billy asked.

The councilman glanced at his watch, sighed quickly, then took the plunge. "Young man, I'm certain you have a fine program and that you personally have the highest intentions. Undoubtedly what you're doing goes very well in the States, but this is England. We have our church, our religion, and we're quite content with things the way they are. We don't want strangers getting up in front of our children with a lot of wild arguments about what they ought to believe."

"I'm afraid you've got us wrong, sir," Billy said. "We didn't come here to argue, but only to explain and, if you don't mind, to pray."

"Those explanations. What personal changes are implicit in them?"

"Only that people accept Christ as their savior and pledge to dedicate their whole lives to Him."

"And then you expect people to go to your church?"

"I have no church," Billy said. "I want people to go to their own churches."

The man slapped his desk impatiently. "Then what is everybody so disturbed about?"

"I don't know," Billy said.

The councilman faced Billy squarely. "Look, young man, I don't like pressures of any kind—not the kind that's been brought to bear the past few days or the kind you've imposed merely by coming into my office, and—"

"I don't mean to pressure you. I only want to explain."

The councilman brushed the interruption aside. "I put it to you this way: as things are, it's almost impossible to bring this matter before the council again unless a majority of the members agree to reconsider it. I doubt that they will. However, if you can organize by yourself such an agreement, I tell you now that I will vote in favor of granting you the permit."

Billy spent the next two days calling on the councilmen. With each, he was humble, direct, patient but firm. He was sympathetic with the delicate position they were in with local groups, and when they detected this they were willing to talk to him openly; only a few were sternly adamant. But enough of them sensed Billy's sincerity and intentions that the matter was once more brought up before the full council. The permit was granted.

There was great rejoicing at the Youth For Christ

headquarters, and in a few the joy of victory was noticeably tinged with arrogance.

Billy was displeased by this. He commented: "If it is so difficult to teach people to love people, how much more difficult it must be to teach people to love God."

Chapter VI

His crusade to imbue people with the love of God—and by it the love of each other—kept Billy traveling almost constantly until mid-1947. Crowds appeared wherever he spoke. At 29, he was hailed as the outstanding evangelist in the country's history. To survive the accolades that flooded Billy required a man of solid character and spiritual substance, both of which Billy possessed. Moreover, he did not measure success by crowds or the number of conversions, but rather by the enduring Christian atmosphere the rallies stimulated. If, months later, he learned that there had been a rise in juvenile delinquency in a past rally-city or even that church attendance by the young had fallen off with time, he instructed his staff to plan a return to the city as soon as possible. Aware of human frailties, Billy was not disheartened by such declines. When he preached about the forgiveness of Christ, he emphasized that Christ was ready to forgive sinners again and again and again—certainly an indication that Christ realized that men would fall and an indication that He would help them rise. Billy was ready to return to any city again and again and again to remind men of this precious blessing.

Each rally brought Billy new followers, new friends, and out of their fondness for him many of them did not hesitate to go to him with their slightest problems. He began to receive hundreds of letters a day, most of them from people he had met only briefly or who had merely been in his audiences. At first he answered all of them personally, sometimes at great length, because he felt that if these people were turning to him for help he was both privileged and obliged to give it. But then the mail reached such proportions that he could not possibly answer it all himself and could not afford sufficient secretaries to answer it. So much of the mail went unanswered, and Billy worried that the writers might feel he did not consider them or their problems worthy of his time. It was one of the plights of popularity on a small budget.

Others of the people Billy attracted did not hesitate to telephone him. While traveling, Billy took as many of the calls as he could, but soon he found them not only interfering with the time needed to prepare his sermons but also interfering with the time required for his own prayers, meditation and Bible-reading. Thereafter he had to monitor the calls in order to control them.

People telephoned him at home. In time, his brief rests at Montreat were spent almost entirely on the telephone: his only defense was to ask the telephone company to give him an unlisted number. This strategy failed when the news circulated that Billy lived across the street from his in-laws. It was soon necessary for the Bells to get an unlisted number. But even this failed. Occasions arose when Billy had to give out his number to the local committee of a future rally-city and it was quickly circulated throughout the country as if it were negotiable. Eventually the Grahams had to have their unlisted number changed after every rally, and so did all the men on his team who were being phoned by people trying to find Billy.

And there were others who did not hesitate to drive right up to the Graham home. In summer, especially, vacationers included a stop at Billy's house on their tours of the South. The first few times this happened, Billy invited the tourists to come in, but this had to be halted when entire busloads appeared at the door. It was embarrassing and disconcerting for the family to be at dinner, for example, and find strangers taking pictures through the window. When Gigi Graham was just two years old, she discovered that visitors were willing to give her a penny to take her picture and a nickel for a guided tour through the rear garden. Gigi's private enterprise flourished for some time, until her mother found out about it.

"If I learn that you have taken another cent from the people," Ruth Graham warned her tiny daughter, "you will never be permitted outside the house again."

Ruth was anxious that her children should have as normal a life as possible. Three years after Gigi, Anne was born, and Ruth was still determined to have at least six children—all of them missionaries. If they were to grow up unaffected by the world attention paid to their father they would have to be protected from the spotlight themselves. As one measure of protection, Ruth sent the children to vacation at Billy's parents' farm during the height of the tourist season.

In the midst of the rush and the fury came an offer that sent Billy's head reeling. He was offered the presidency of a college.

ii

No two lives could differ more than those of an evangelist and a college president. Billy knew this. The offer therefore baffled and amused him.

It had come from Dr. W. B. Riley of Minneapolis. Once a popular evangelist himself, Riley had founded the Northwestern Bible School in 1902. Over the years the school expanded into a Baptist seminary and then into a liberal arts college. Riley was now an old man and suspected he was not long for this world. Concerned about the institution which had been his life's work, he was anxious to find the best man available to succeed him. After a cautious survey of the field, he chose Billy.

"Me a college president?" Billy put the question to Ruth. "I'm not equipped for a job like that. In the first place, all I've got is a bachelor's degree. In the second place, I couldn't sit still long enough for such a job. Honey, I'm an evangelist, now and from now on."

He wrote Riley that he was highly honored by the offer but that he could not possibly accept it.

Riley refused to accept a refusal. He sent Billy a long letter, replete with Bible quotations, arguing that he was convinced it was God's Will that Billy should take over the college. Furthermore, he said, the school turned out evangelists and since Billy was the best evangelist in the country he ought to be concerned about future evangelists.

Again Billy refused, saying: "My schedule for Youth For Christ rallies does not permit me to take on other work, regardless of how important that work may be."

Riley replied: "You can do both. You can work for Youth For Christ four days a week and for the college three days a week. I truly believe this is God's Will for you and that He will send you a sign. Please let me have your favorable decision by commencement, 1947, so I can inform the board of directors."

In May, Billy wrote Riley that he was still uncertain; he asked for more time to make a decision. In July he wrote that: "I have been waiting for Heaven's signal. I have not received it as yet."

In August, Riley, convinced that he was dying, begged Billy to go to Minneapolis, if only for a talk. Billy went. He was welcomed by an ill but stern old man who had his decisive argument ready.

"Do you know," Riley asked, "how David got to be king of Israel?"

"Yes," said Billy. "He was appointed by the prophet Samuel."

"Under those conditions, he could not refuse, could he?"

"Hardly."

"Very well," said Riley. "I hereby appoint you the president of this school. And you can't refuse. I will meet you at the judgment seat of Christ to see what kind of job you did."

Put that way, Billy felt he could not refuse. He took

the position, knowing he was surrendering the last free hours he had for himself and his family. It was a frantic existence. His personal popularity attracted much attention to the school, which meant added work for him. As president, he was responsible for raising funds, and this meant that on his travels for rallies he had also to call on successful alumni for donations. Enrollments increased, which meant planning new dormitories, new classrooms, new student programs.

Billy's personal stature increased as well. In light of his position in education, he was granted a doctorate in divinity by Kings College in 1948. In 1950, Houghton College awarded him an honorary doctorate of laws. He could now call himself Doctor Billy Graham—which was a long way from the little boy who milked cows at three o'clock in the morning on a North Carolina farm.

Also increasing were the requests for him to address adult groups. In many cases, the requests came from other evangelists who found themselves confronted with important revivals that required a speaker of Billy's calibre. Inadvertently, then, Billy was moving back into the type of evangelism where he had started and which he much preferred.

But there were only 24 hours in the day. The school, Youth For Christ, the revivals, the mail, lectures—there was simply too much to do. The time came when Billy had to decide which of his many projects he had to give up. Of them all, Youth For Christ seemed in least need of him. It was running smoothly and effectively; new men had come along and were doing excellent work. If the organization needed him, Billy could attend major rallies. Freed of the great number of local rallies, he could give more to evangelism among adults.

This was the work he had believed that God intended for him; he believed it all his life. It was the work he knew best, did best, loved best. Having now earned an international reputation, he felt he was ready to go into evangelism on a broad scale. Revivals, Billy observed, were too often restricted to small towns or to cities where a rural population had migrated, all of which gave the impression that revivals were intended only for farmers. Billy did not believe this should be the case. Revivals were exactly what they were called: an effort to revive the faith. As such, they ought to encompass everybody. The sophisticated New Yorker, the Chicago steel worker, the Los Angeles movie-studio employee needed revivals as much as anybody else. The trick would be to make the proper approach. After all, Youth For Christ rallies had succeeded in big cities; revivals could, too.

With this in mind, Billy began to organize a team. He asked Cliff Barrows to join him as director of music and George Beverly Shea to be his featured soloist. At Northwestern Bible School was a young professor of theology and Hebrew named Jerry Beaven who had expressed an interest in evangelism; Billy took him on as promotion director. Then Billy reached back into his boyhood for his old friend Grady Wilson, who had spent the intervening years at church work in the South.

In the summer of 1949, the team began, charting a tour that would take them eastward to Baltimore, then across the country to Los Angeles. It was an ambitious tour, penetrating areas mostly untouched by revivals. The team was very hopeful.

They started off well enough, encouraged if not by enormous crowds at least by satisfactory responses to the altar call. At Baltimore they rented the Lyric Theater, a bold gesture because of the theater's 2800-capacity. They drew good crowds, but the theater was never quite filled. An hour before the closing meeting they held a private prayer session, asking for a full audience, but the prayer was not answered. They found various ways to console themselves: they were new, they were pioneering a virgin field, many city-dwellers were away on vacations, some hardened city editors had not given them enough publicity, they lacked funds for an all-out advertising campaign.

And now Los Angeles.

If they had trouble filling the 2800 seats of the Baltimore theater, they wondered how on earth they were going to fill the 6000-seat tent they were to use at Los Angeles. A number of Southerners had moved to Los

Angeles to work in the city's huge factories; they knew what a revival was and surely a good percentage would attend. But would they fill the giant tent?

Grady Wilson had gone on ahead to make preliminary arrangements. He was relieved when he encountered no more than the usual number of noncommital clergymen who preferred not to have the revival in their city and displayed their attitude by a lack of cooperation. Among laymen, Grady found more encouraging support. Prayer groups were started to pray for the revival's success and to arouse attendance.

When Billy arrived, Grady admitted: "That tent still looks as big as ever, Billy."

It stood at the corner of Washington and Hill streets in the downtown section of the city. They had rented it for three weeks. It was expensive.

The first-night audience was good. The tent wasn't filled but, all things considered, they hadn't expected that. They hoped, however, that word-of-mouth news of them would spread and the attendance would pick up. But on the second night the crowd was even smaller.

"We need some prayers, Grady," Billy said. "Get those groups of yours busy."

For the rest of the week, Grady spent all day touring the vast Los Angeles area, begging for prayers. On his drives he realized that one of the problems was the size of the city itself. Downtown in Los Agneles didn't mean what it meant elsewhere. People did not flock downtown every evening to shop or attend movies. Every outlying section had its own downtown, closer and more convenient, and every suburb was the same. Moreover, most of the factory workers had to be on their jobs early; returning to their distant homes so late from the revival imposed a hardship they could not be expected to endure every night.

But Billy kept insisting: "More prayers, more prayers."

Toward the end of the week the attendance rose slightly but was still below what it should have been. Night after night, Billy faced disappointing rows of empty seats. The second week was about the same. Sufficient donations came in from the audiences to meet expenses, but there was nothing left over to provide the necessary down-payment on the tent or arena of the next town.

As the second week ended, Billy and Grady held a conference. "We've got to decide whether we'll stay on for the third week," Grady said.

"I'd hate to quit," said Billy. "We must be doing some good here. Even one conversion a night would make it worth while."

"Of course," Grady agreed, "but we can't overlook the financial aspect of all this. We went in the hole in Baltimore and we're really going to be in bad shape here if things don't pick up."

"How I dislike discussing money," Billy admitted. "I remember the first time I got paid for preaching in Florida; I was appalled. I appreciate the problem, Grady, but I just can't bring myself to talk about money and religion in the same breath."

"Unfortunately we have to," said Grady. "Now, what do you want to do here?"

"I want to stay."

"Okay. We stay."

At the outset, the third week followed the same discouraging pattern. Desperately, the prayer groups continued their prayers.

There were other factors at work.

Every night reporters attended the meetings. They did not come with enthusiasm or even particular interest; there was a revival in town, a newsworthy note in itself, and somebody had to cover it. Back at their desks after each meeting, the reporters wrote short articles, perhaps three or four inches long, about what Billy had said and about the size of the crowd. The article was usually printed in the back of the paper with other religious news.

Up north in California, in his magnificent estate called San Simeon, William Randolph Hearst made a daily habit of studying the final editions of all the newspapers he owned across the country. In his office was a teletype machine, connecting him with the score of editorial offices of his domain. To the many editors, the Chief's machine, as it was called, was something of an altar, and when the receiver in their offices began to ring its bell and tap out messages the editors trembled: Hearst seldom contacted them unless he had a complaint.

One morning toward the end of Billy's third dismal week in Los Angeles, Hearst happened to notice a small item on the back pages of his Los Angeles papers about the revival. Hearst had never met Billy, but he knew about Billy's work with the Youth For Christ movement and strongly approved it. He wondered why Billy wasn't getting better coverage in Los Angeles. He rang for his secretary and the woman came into the spacious office.

Hearst said: "Send a message to the Los Angeles editors."

"Yes, sir?"

"Puff Graham."

That was it.

But it was not all.

Across the country in the New York offices of *Time Magazine,* Publisher Henry Luce was going over the daily summary of news items from his reports around the world. He noticed, as he had for the past two weeks, that Billy Graham was holding a revival in Los Angeles, and he remembered that he had seen nothing more about it than the mere announcement. *Time* had printed articles about Youth For Christ and they had drawn good response. Luce instructed the editor with him: "Tell the religious department to get something on Graham out in California."

Thus two of the world's most important publishers turned their attention to Billy Graham almost simultaneously. The prayers of the Los Angeles groups traveled thousands of miles to make themselves heard at home.

iii

That night when Billy arrived at the tent he was surprised to see that the press section was over-crowded. "What's going on?" he asked Grady.

"I don't know," Grady said. "I'm just sorry we can't take up a collection among the reporters, there's so many of them."

"Any explanations at all?"

"Well, the Hearst men showed up en masse, and when the other reporters saw that they called their offices for help. Then the *Time* people arrived; they haven't been here before. Anything special happen to you today?"

"No," Billy said. "But it must have happened to somebody else."

The next day Billy was front-page news. His sermon was reported in deatil, there were pictures of him preaching and pictures of those who answered his altar call. Billy was overwhelmed by all the attention and a little amused by it. "You'd think this was the first revival ever held," he said.

It seemed so. That night the tent was packed, and the overflow crowd on the streets was so big that loudspeakers had to be installed for them. The next night was the same, and so was the next. Whatever reasons people had for not attending the revival earlier they put aside. Recalcitrant ministers discarded their objections either to Billy or the revival and urged their people to go. Prayer groups switched from petitory prayers to prayers of gratitude. On the last night, a torrent of telegrams arrived, asking Billy to stay on.

He stayed five weeks.

Everyday he was front-page news.

Surely there were important moments in Billy's past, moments that touched the heart and the soul, but nothing was quite as exciting as the extended five weeks of the Los Angeles crusade. The great crowds, the numerous conversions, the wave of spirituality that swept across the city all combined to produce a religious event unique in the history of the country. A part of the world, famous for its celluloid make-believe, did a realistic about-face and turned to God. Movie stars, noted athletes, even underworld hoods responded to Billy's invitation to make decisions for Christ. The daily papers carried profiles of the converts, the uncelebrated as well as the celebrated.

The usual reluctance of people to discuss their religious experiences disappeared: those who had chosen God were ready to proclaim their decisions to the world. In doing so, they overcame the hesitance of others poised at the same moment of decision.

Billy shunned all efforts to make a celebrity out of himself. "This spiritual adventure in Los Angeles is not my doing, but God's," he insisted. "I am merely His tool. If God should take His hand off me, my lips would turn to clay."

A reporter asked: "Can you tell us why God has chosen you to be His tool?"

Billy shook his head and grinned. "I don't know. When I get to Heaven that's the first question I'm going to ask Him."

"You don't deny," another reporter asked, "that most people are coming to the crusade because they have heard so much about you and want to see what you're like?"

"If I'm a curiosity people want to stare at, that's all right with me," Billy said. "Just so they listen to what God gives me to say. This is the important thing: the Bible says God will not share His glory with anyone. Any preacher who gets the idea that he is more important than God's message is making a great mistake. If I ever find I have acquired that idea I will give up the ministry because I will have ceased being God's servant and tried to make Him mine."

This was the kind of honest self-appraisal that gave Billy Graham the sincerity that attracted thousands to him. Recognizing it, they knew they could confide in him, trust him, follow him, knowing that his only interest was to lead them where he himself wanted to go: to God.

The Los Angeles crusade could have gone on for months. It might well, in fact, have become a permanent California fixture. But there were other commitments Billy had made in other cities and it was necessary for him to be on his way. Before leaving Los Angeles, Billy heard talk that Las Vegas gamblers were betting ten-to-one that the results of the crusade would fade as soon as Billy was out of the city. This perturbed him. He cared little whether or not he was a flash in the pan, but he did not want the vital decisions of the converts to be. As he left the city, he said:

"God has blessed Los Angeles. It is not the same city it was two months ago. You owe it to God and yourselves to see that Los Angeles remains what it now is. Otherwise, all that has been done here will have been in vain."

He need not have worried. In the dozen years that followed, Los Angeles friends kept him informed: the churches remained filled, the converts remained steadfast, the spirituality Billy had stirred remained high. The Las Vegas gamblers paid off.

Billy had hoped to be able to go to Montreat for a brief vacation with his family but the extension of the Los Angeles crusade prevented that. Eager to see his family, Billy asked Ruth if she would like to spend a few days with him in Boston, the next crusade city. She said she would and that she would bring Gigi along. They all met in New York, had a day to themselves, then took the train to Boston.

A battalion of reporters met the train. Never had Billy been given such a reception. Undeniably, he was now Big Time. Outside the station, an enormous crowd surrounded the car that awaited him. When the crowd saw him, a cheer went up, people called out his name and applauded him; one group began to sing a hymn. Billy paused a moment and looked out over the crowd. He was deeply touched, but at the same time he was wary of the adulation.

Gazing at the crowd, he whispered: "This is for you, God, for you."

After checking into their hotel, Billy and Ruth went to crusade headquarters for a press conference, to be briefed on the latest developments and to meet the local volunteers. The suite of offices roared with activity. As they moved from room to room, Billy shook hands with the volunteers and thanked them for all they had done. It was as they were entering the last room that Billy recognized one of the women-workers, and his heart stopped.

Ruth saw Billy's reaction and she knew instinctively who the woman must be. She went to the woman and took her hand.

"I've been wanting to meet you for years," Ruth said. "May I say something personal to you? Like any girl, when I was young I prayed that someday I would find the perfect husband, and I know now that I've done so. I have you to thank for it, for if you had accepted Billy when he proposed to you at the Florida school he would not be mine now."

The woman who once expressed the opinion that Billy Graham would never amount to anything returned Ruth's firm grasp and said: "I'm glad you are happy."

Ruth felt Billy's arm embrace her. She could not remember when she had been quite so happy.

Chapter VII

Now the demands on Billy grew. Not only were there rallies and crusades to be conducted in major cities across the land, but there were, as well, Bible conferences, ministerial conventions and lay seminars. There was still the Northwestern Bible School in Minneapolis, and requests began to pour in for Billy to write articles and books. The mail continued heavy, and so did the long-distance telephone calls. The mere process of fulfilling his vocation was turning Billy into a national institution. He wondered how long he could go on until he drowned in the flood of things that had to be done.

He took care to protect his health by escaping to the peace of Montreat whenever he could. While traveling, he welcomed occasions that would get him away from the pressure of the moment. His face was now as familiar to the general public as the President's; it was impossible for him to go anywhere without being recognized and approached. To have a little time for himself, therefore, became not only a necessity but a rare treat.

One summer day in 1950, while attending a conference of ministers at Ocean City, New Jersey, the occasion of a little privacy arose unexpectedly when a minister asked Billy if he would like to go for a drive. "I thought you'd like to have a few hours off," the man said.

"That's very considerate of you," said Billy. "I need exactly that."

They drove south along the coast, at times catching glimpses of the sea and at other times moving through the quiet streets of resort towns. They chatted when they felt like it and drove along in silence when they felt like that. It was a beautiful day, warm and sunny, and Billy could feel the needed relaxation seeping through his lean frame.

Lunch time came. They stopped at a roadside diner and went in, sat down and ordered. They were just about to start eating when Billy heard: "This is surely God's doing." Billy looked up. At his elbow was a man dressed in a cleric's suit. "I must talk to you," the man said. He introduced himself; he was a minister from Philadelphia. Billy invited him to sit down.

"Last night," the preacher said, "I awoke suddenly and found myself thinking of you."

Billy grinned. "Nightmare?"

But the man was too serious. "I can't explain why," he said, "but I couldn't get the idea out of my mind that you should be on radio, on a network, and that it was my job to put you there."

"I used to have a program in Chicago," Billy said.

"You should be on the networks," the preacher said. "The whole country should hear your message regularly."

"That takes a lot of money," Billy said, "and I haven't got it. And it takes time, something else I haven't much of these days."

The minister brushed the objections aside. "All that can be arranged. This is God's will, Doctor Graham; I'm sure of it. When I awoke thinking about you last night, I thought you were in Europe. I didn't know what in the world I could do about this idea, how I could reach you to put it to you. This morning I was so preoccupied with the plan that I couldn't concentrate on my own work, so I went for a drive, hoping to clear my mind. Then here, in this roadside diner, of all places, I encounter you. You can't say that all this is merely coincidence. God's will is certainly evident."

"It's an impressive experience," Billy conceded. "Believe me, I never question things like this because they can well be God's will. But, truthfully, a radio program is the farthest thing from my mind. I haven't the money, the time or the organization for it, I don't know anybody at the networks, I wouldn't even know how to begin."

"Never mind," the man said. "Everything will work out. Now, I'm sorry I interrupted your lunch; I'll leave you alone now. But you haven't heard the last of this idea. Mark my words." And he left.

The minister with Billy shook his head. "Does this happen to you often?"

"Not exactly like this, but people are always coming up to me," Billy said. "But I don't mind. This radio idea, of course, is extremely remote, but usually people only want to talk about some problem they have. If I can help, I'm grateful. With something like this, there's nothing I can do."

He put the incident out of his mind. Two weeks later, as president of the college, he attended a conference of educators in Northern Michigan. In the midst of it, he was told he had two visitors. He went out to meet them. They were Walter Bennett, president of his own advertising agency in Chicago, and Fred Dienert, Bennett's associate from Philadelphia.

"You met my pastor in New Jersey recently," Dienert said. "He talked to you about a network radio program."

"Oh, yes," Billy said.

"That's why we're here," Bennett said. "We'd like to discuss it with you."

"I'm afraid," said Billy, "that there's nothing to discuss. Really, my schedule is overcrowded as it is; I haven't time for a radio program. And in the second place—forgive me for being blunt—I simply am not interested."

A week later Billy was at Montreat. The doorbell rang, and when Billy answered it there stood Bennett and Dienert. "You two sure are persistent," Billy observed. "Come on in, but I'll tell you now you're wasting your time."

"We've looked further into the idea," Bennett explained when they were all seated in Billy's study. "We can get an hour on Sunday afternoon, thirteen weeks coast to coast, for $92,000."

Billy guffawed. "I haven't got money like that," he said. "I can't even conceive of that much money. Why don't we just forget about all this?"

In another week Billy was out in Portland, Oregon, for a crusade. His fame had traveled ahead of him. On the first night, 18,000 people turned out to hear him, and the attendance held at that night after night. Day after day, telephone calls and telegrams came from Bennett and Dienert urging Billy to reconsider the idea of a network program. Billy was getting annoyed. Then Bennett and Dienert flew to Portland in another effort to convince him to change his mind.

"No," Billy said. "No."

Bennett said: "The network has offered a new arrangement for payment. If $25,000 can be raised for a downpayment, it will be possible to pay the rest at approximately $7,000 a week."

Billy could not help but laugh. "You have no idea how fantastic those figures sound to me," he said. "It's out of the question, fellows."

Dienert suggested: "You could ask for donations. On a network hookup, you ought to be able to raise $7,000 a week."

"Years ago," Billy said, "I was scared to death just trying to raise $150 a week to pay for a radio program."

"Times have changed," Dienert pointed out.

"Not that much," Billy said.

The advertising men remained in Portland two days,

catching Billy on the run whenever they could to press him for a reconsideration, but he would not change his mind. At last they sent word to him that they were giving up. Billy invited them to his room to say good-bye.

Bennett was depressed. "I still think it's wrong not to give the idea a try, at least."

Dienert felt the same. "My pastor's got me convinced that this program is God's will. Frankly, I don't like shelving the project in the face of something like that."

Billy tried to console them. "Sometimes it's difficult to perceive what God's will is. But my experience has been that there is always a sign. Something happens. Regardless of how coincidental it may seem, something happens. In this case, I have sensed nothing."

"Have you asked for a sign?" Dienert asked.

"No," Billy said, "as a matter of fact, I haven't. Very well, then. You two have certainly done all you could. Let's pray together and ask God to let us know if He wants this program to go through."

They all knelt. Billy was rather apprehensive; personally he disapproved of putting God to a test by asking for a sign, but he felt there was nothing else he could do in order to settle the matter. His prayer was short. He said: "Heavenly Father, you know the question that is facing us. We want to do your will. If it is your desire that we should do this program, let us know in anyway you wish. Your will be done, Lord, not mine."

In a few minutes, Billy was saying good-bye to Bennett and Dienert, both of whom promised Billy they would never annoy him with future efforts to change his mind. "We will accept the answer to your prayer," Bennett said. He and Dienert checked out of the hotel and went to the airport.

Billy went to the crusade meeting. In his sermon, he touched on the subject of prayer, explaining that it was through prayer that men communicated their needs to God and it was the way in which God reacted to prayers that He let men know His plans for them. Billy said:

"I want all of you to pray for me tonight. I'll tell you why. For the past few weeks, two men from back East have been following me around the country with the idea that I ought to go on a radio network every Sunday and preach God's message to the whole country. These are fine men, good Christian men, and they feel that this program is God's will, God's plan for me and my ministry for Him. Now, I haven't been very favorable toward this idea since it first came up. The main problem is that it costs a lot of money, much more money than I have, and if I ever had that much money I'm not sure I'd spend it on a radio program. Now the question we're facing is what is God's will. Don't worry. I'm not going to ask you for money. But I am going to ask you for prayers. I'm going to ask you to pray for me tonight, asking God to let me know what He wants me to do."

He went on with his sermon. Finishing, he went into an office to talk for a moment with those who had responded to his altar call. Then he went to the crusade office. Outside it he saw a long line of people. He went into the office and saw Grady Wilson staring down unbelieving at a shoe box full of money and slips of paper.

"What's all this?" Billy asked.

"Donations," said Grady. "For the radio program."

Billy was speechless.

"Look," Grady said, "cash, checks, pledges. There must be thousands here. And it's still coming in."

At last Billy said: "This is amazing. I didn't ask for money. I didn't say anything about my prayer this afternoon. I didn't even indicate how much I needed."

When they finally counted the money, the total was $23,500.

Grady said: "Well, that's it. You couldn't ask for a clearer answer to your prayer."

"I could," Billy said, to Grady's surprise. "Remember, the Devil could raise $23,500 just as easily as God. My prayer was for $25,000, and we didn't get that much."

Bennett and Dienert walked in. Billy said: "I thought you were on a plane."

Bennett said: "We found we could get a later one tonight, so we came back for the meeting." He saw the pile of money and gave Billy an inquiring look.

Billy said: "You heard my remarks, then, about the radio program. That's the results. There's $23,500 in cash and pledges."

"Wonderful!" Bennett said. "Fred Dienert and I will put up the remaining $1,500, then we're in business."

"Oh no we're not," Billy said. "We prayed for $25,000, and $25,000 it's got to be." He prepared to go back to his hotel.

Grady asked: "What are we going to do with all this money? The banks are closed, so we can't deposit it."

"You'll have to keep an eye on it," Billy said. "And I hope you made a list of the contributors because we may have to give it all back."

Bennett was annoyed. "Billy, these people want you to go on the air. Are you going to disappoint them merely because you're a few pennies short?"

"Only the full $25,000 will assure me this is God's will," Billy said flatly.

He left the office. Grady scooped all the money and pledges into the shoe box and followed him. Bennett and Dienert were at Billy's heels, arguing. They followed him and Grady into a taxi and drove with them to the hotel, arguing all the way. Billy did not listen to them. At the hotel, he went to the reception desk and asked for his key. He was given his key and three letters.

He turned to Bennett. "I'll say good-bye to you here. I'm very tired and don't want to sit up tonight."

"Listen," Bennett said, beginning his argument again.

Billy opened one of the envelopes and glanced at its contents. "No," he said. "You listen." Then he read: "I am a farmer here in Oregon, too far from Portland to attend your crusade. But I think it would be wonderful if I could hear you on the radio. So I am sending you my check for a thousand dollars as a starter for what I hope will be the Billy Graham Radio Fund."

The four men looked at each other. Grady said: "That makes it $24,500."

Billy opened the other two envelopes. Each contained a check for $250; on one was written: "The line at the crusade was too long, so I brought my donation to your hotel."

"You know what that makes it?" Bennett asked pointedly.

"A miracle," Billy said. "All right, come on upstairs. I guess I will be up late after all."

"We've got a lot of talking to do," Bennett said.

Billy corrected him. "We've got a lot of praying to do."

ii

Among the more staid religionists, the question often arose: "Precisely what does Billy Graham believe?"

Billy himself had answered the question when he said: "I believe in the inspiration of the Holy Bible, the Virgin Birth, the resurrection of the Christ from the grave, the atonement by His blood of the sins of mankind, and the return of Christ to establish a kingdom on earth."

It was a crisp credo, a fundamental credo, encompassing the basic beliefs held by most Christians for centuries. And Billy made no compromise with any part of it. A Protestant himself and appealing primarily to Protestants, Billy nevertheless addressed himself to the world. He believed that the answer to every personal or universal problem could be found only in Christ, and he said so out loud wherever he was.

Sometimes there were Jews in his audiences; certainly Jews heard his national radio program and, later watched him on television. Aware that he was treading on their sensitivities, he nonetheless spoke to them as he did all men, urging them to make the decision many of their forefathers had made two thousand years earlier: Accept Christ. How many actually did, Billy would never know, but from his mail he learned that his pleas were stirring positive responses.

The same was true of Catholics. On various occasions, the Catholic hierarchy directed Catholic laymen not to attend Billy's crusades. Without discrediting the man himself, the bishops pointed out that the crusade sessions were actually religious services, worship, and as such Catholics were not to partake in them. This was established Catholic attitude and would have held no matter who the Protestant preacher might be. The bishops also said that although Billy put forth many excellent ideas in his sermons the fact remained that, for Catholics at least, salvation was not alone in the acceptance of Christ as savior but ineluctably in the participation in the sacraments, of which historically the Catholic Church claimed to be the sole valid guardian.

Billy regretted the occasions when the Catholic issue arose. Once when addressing a social club in New York he recognized in the audience Father James Keller, founder of the Christopher Movement, the Catholic project which advocated that one Christian carrying out his obligations could change the world. Looking at Father Keller with sincerity and affection, Billy told of an experience he had at a crusade when the arena lights went out. Someone in the audience lighted a match. Billy obtained matches and lighted one, and he said to the crowd: "You light your light and I'll light mine and together we can light up the world." The New York clubmembers got his point and applauded.

Despite the Catholic stand, Billy knew he had Catholics among his followers. They listened to his programs and wrote him; they came to the crusades and responded to his altar calls. In both instances, he sent them on to their own pastors.

Sending people on to their own churches was a regular practice in Billy's work by the time of the Portland crusade in 1950. It was a new idea in evangelism; it gave evangelism roots. It worked this way: a few weeks before a particular crusade, an advance team would arrive. There was always much work to be done—final arrangements on renting an arena, obtaining a choir, setting up offices and living quarters, acquiring buses to bring in suburban residents, conferences with ministers and laymen, publicity—the list was long. During this period, laymen were interviewed, usually by Grady Wilson, to qualify as counselors. They had to be model Christians themselves, and if they had experience in personnel work or executive capacities so much the better. They were to have two jobs during the crusade. They were to take specified places in the arena shortly before the altar call in order to help people who might be undergoing too great an emotional trial in making their decisions for Christ. Afterwards, they were to go to the counseling offices where those who had made their decisions would be brought to them. Interviews with the converts were usually brief. Knowing the city, the counselors could recommend a church to the convert where he could go for particular guidance by an ordained minister. A card was then sent to the ministers, advising them that the convert would come for a visit on a particular date and urging them to seek out the convert in the event that he failed to appear. Thus pastoral work was left where it belonged: in the hands of pastors. If by chance the convert wanted immediate guidance, most counselors were qualified to give it. In any case, several local ministers were nearby to assist if necessary. Before leaving, the convert was given a Bible and other spiritual reading.

It was by this method of forging a link between the individual and the church of his choice that Billy Graham achieved lasting results. Billy felt that church-attendance was essential in the fulfillment of a conversion and when obdurate churchmen realized this they invariably mellowed whatever objections they had to him.

The word "convert" bothered many churchmen. To them it indicated a change, usually from one denomination to another, and it became necessary for Billy to clarify his interpretation of the word.

He said: "The Bible says that unless ye be converted ye shall not be saved. The word convert means to turn to. So unless you turn to Christ dramatically and completely you will be damned."

It was possible, Billy said, that for some people the act of spiritual conversion would not be very dramatic. His own wife admitted that she never had the experience, but certainly Ruth was a true and vivid Christian.

Raised in a very religious home, she took on her spiritual convictions in the normal process of growing up; for her no moment of turning was involved. But most people, Billy said, were not that fortunate. For most there had to be a moment of turning, a moment of decision. It could happen anywhere, anytime—in church, at a crusade rally, at home listening to a radio sermon, on the job, walking the street, even in an atmosphere of temptation.

"Nobody has to tell you whether or not you are living for Christ," Billy once said. "You know whether you are, and you may be the only human being who knows it. Despite the old adage, it really is possible to fool most of the people most of the time. But you can't fool Christ. The day you realize that is the day your salvation begins, because if you realize it and do nothing about it, your own common sense will tell you that you are asking for hell."

In any event, because the word convert proved troublesome in a few quarters Billy gradually dropped it and adopted the term Inquirer—a person who came forward asking after Christ.

References to hell and sin jarred some of Billy's listeners, but he did not care. "We have pussyfooted long enough in our religion," Billy said. "It's time we face the facts."

The facts as Billy saw them were in the Bible, which he quoted continually, which was in his hands so often, which was always within his arm's reach.

Accepting the Bible wholly and literally, Billy believed entirely in the history of the world as related in Genesis. He believed that one day God told the angels that, at a given time in the future, His Son would become man, would offer up His manhood to atone for the sins of the world and would thereafter be the judge of all men, thus ruler of the world. Then, Billy believed, the archangel Lucifer resented surrendering his own jurisdiction over the world, he rebelled and, with his followers, was rejected from heaven. Thereafter they became the creatures known as devils who roam the world attempting to attract souls away from the saving influence of God. Believing this, Billy also believed that Adam and Eve were indeed the first human beings, that they disobeyed God, for which sin they were evicted from the Garden of Eden, and that it was to atone for this original sin that Jesus Christ became man and underwent His crucifixion. All evil, Billy believed, issued from the sin of Adam and Eve, and it would be only by the complete return of all mankind to Christ that evil would disappear. Only then would the Kingdom of God on earth be possible; until then, those who sinned would suffer.

But it had become unfashionable to believe in devils or hell, for to do so one would also have to admit the existence of sin and concede that one might at times be guilty of it, that one had offended God and was thus deserving of punishment. Sophisticates were willing to grant that the Ten Commandments existed and that they ought to be obeyed, but they said that the bad thing about breaking the Commandments was that it resulted in a personality change, caused by a sense of guilt, that made the violator a case for a psychiatrist.

Billy Graham would have no part of that. Holding up a Bible, he said:

"Here it is—the source of everything Christians believe. This is the book that records God's laws and His promise of redemption. But you can't pick and choose with this book—you either accept it all or reject it all. You can't just believe what's convenient for you and reject what is inconvenient and think you are going to be saved. We have a Constitution in this country that exists for the good of all. If any man tries to interpret the Constitution to please himself or suit his own ends, he'll get in trouble. It may take a little time for the law to catch up with him, but it will. The same is true of the Bible. It was given to us for the good of all, but if we try to juggle it around to find excuses for ourselves we'll be in trouble. If we don't want to live according to the Constitution, we can move out of the country. If we don't want to live according to the Bible—the whole Bible, well,

God has prepared a place for us to move and I guarantee you that's where we'll end up."

Accepting the Bible, Billy said, was an act of faith. He had an anecdote to demonstrate just what that faith involved.

"You've heard," he once said in a sermon, "about the acrobat who walks back and forth over Niagara Falls on a tightrope. Well, he was up there one day, gliding back and forth gracefully and skillfully, amazing the crowd that was watching him. Then he put the wheel of a wheelbarrow on the rope and pushed that over to Canada and back. The crowd gave him a big hand for that and thought the man was wonderful. Then he filled the wheelbarrow with dirt and pushed that over the Falls and back without any trouble. When he got back to the crowd, he said: 'You've all seen me cross the Falls several times, even push a wheel-barrow full of dirt. Do you believe your eyes? Do you believe I can do this over and over?' The crowd said: 'Yes, sir, we saw and we believe. You sure are a wonderful acrobat.' And the acrobat said: 'All right, then. I'm going to make one more round-trip with the wheel-barrow, but I'd like a passenger. Will a volunteer kindly step forward to ride in the wheel-barrow on the tightrope over to Canada and back?' Do you think he got a volunteer? Why, I tell you those people were back in Buffalo so fast they didn't even stir up the dirt on the road. That's the way too many people are with God, with the Bible. Everything's fine until they're personally involved, then they pick up and run, they back off. If anybody in that crowd at Niagara Falls really had faith, really believed in the ability of the acrobat, he would have climbed into the wheel-barrow and enjoyed the ride of his life. It's the same with God. If you really believe in Him, have faith in Him and in His promise to the world as revealed by Him in the Bible, and if your trust in Him is carried out by the way you obey Him in your daily life, then you can enjoy the ride of your life—straight to heaven!"

So if there was any question about what Billy Graham believed the most obvious answer was that he believed the Bible—with no ifs, ands or buts. He believed, too, that the duties implied in the Bible could be carried out in daily life with the graces of God and a few simple methods.

He urged people to practice humility, to recognize their dependence on God, that without Him they would be nothing. Acceptance of Jesus Christ as savior, he said, must be paired with a definite and vivid trust in Him, demonstrated by heeding His admonitions. Penitance was important, Billy believed; moreover, it was vital to the forgiveness of sins. The practice of virtues was, Billy often said, Christianity in action. He said the best code of conduct was the Beatitudes; a highlight in some of his crusades was a sermon each night on one of the Beatitudes.

"Be filled with the Spirit," he frequently preached. To do so, one had only to display the gifts of the Spirit: love, joy, peace, long-suffering gentleness, goodness, faith, meekness, temperance. These gifts, he said, were every Christian's, but by letting selfishness and sin prevent the practice of them the Christian forced the Holy Spirit completely out of his life.

And he said: "Pray, read the Bible, meditate, develop the daily habit of spiritual tastes. Love your neighbor, love God, and remember always that you are immortal and will live forever in the next world of your own choosing."

Billy knew the next world he had chosen. And he wanted everybody in this world to go there with him.

Chapter VIII

The response to the network radio program awakened Billy to the need of further organization of his work. Already he had been criticized for being over-organized;

the skill with which his team entered a city and prepared for a revival and carried it off struck some people as having too great a resemblance to big business. To this Billy responded: "I am in a big business—the big business of saving souls. I am selling the most important product in the world—salvation. Why shouldn't it be as much promoted as a campaign to sell soap?"

But now even more organization was required. From the start, the radio program brought in over 10,000 letters a week. As in Western Springs, some of the letters contained contributions, but most of them requested personal guidance. The mere physical task of opening the mail demanded a staff; providing the guidance demanded a battalion of qualified clergymen.

Billy himself needed organization. Early in 1951, he said: "I am trying to do the work of ten men, and if I don't watch myself I'll end up not doing any of the jobs well."

His first step was to resign the presidency of the Minneapolis school. In the process of doing so, Billy discussed his problems with George Wilson, one of the minister-professors of the school. "I need someone who has a mind for business matters," Billy said, "someone who at the same time has a mind for spiritual matters."

"That shouldn't be too hard to find," Wilson said.

"Maybe not," Billy conceded, "but it will also have to be someone who's willing to work cheap."

Wilson laughed. "I've worked cheap all my life, but not because I've been willing to. Such is the plight of a preacher-teacher."

Billy looked at Wilson with new eyes. "George, what about you for this job?"

"Handling your paper-work?"

"Yes."

Wilson shrugged. "I've never done anything like that."

"But I'm sure you can," Billy assured.

"I'll try, if you want me to, and if you're not satisfied you can fire me."

"Fine," said Billy, "and if you're not satisfied you can fire me."

With that, the Billy Graham Evangelistic Association, Inc., was established, with offices in Minneapolis. The first offices were three rooms, housing Wilson and one secretary. Billy was president of the association, Grady Wilson acted as vice president, George Wilson (no relation) became secretary-treasurer, and Cliff Barrows and Ruth Graham were made members of the board. Within five years, the association grew to a staff of 125, including a nucleus of qualified laymen who answered the "problem" mail, all housed in a four-story building equipped with the latest machinery for their highly specialized work.

George Wilson actually supervised the association, and of all his work the letters seeking guidance was the most important. After months of study, he discovered that the subject of the letters fell into 40 specific categories. At one time or another, Billy had discussed the subjects in his sermons. From the sermons, therefore, Wilson was able to prepare answers for each subject, a method which cut down the work considerably. Even so, there were letters for which there could be no generalized response, and these Wilson answered himself, soberly aware of the tremendous responsibility involved.

The radio program, called *Hour of Decision,* provided the association with most of its operating funds. Although there had been one donation of $50,000, most of them were under three dollars, and these were so irregular that occasionally Wilson was forced to send out letters of appeal to past contributors. Early in the association's history, a second office was opened in Washington, D. C., for the production of religious movies to be rented to church groups at a small fee, often for no fee at all. Invariably the film program ran up a deficit every year, but because of the importance of the movies the bills were paid out of the radio-listener donations.

Billy Graham never outgrew his reluctance to accept money for doing God's work. The surprise he had expressed on being paid for the first time by the small Florida church remained with him throughout the years. He took no money for the revivals he conducted between leaving Florida and going to Western Springs, his salary at Western Springs scarcely kept him and Ruth alive, and his pay, while with Youth For Christ, was not much better.

When, in the late Forties, he began his own crusades across the country, he took no stipulated salary. The crusades themselves were expensive, absorbing most of what audiences donated, and Billy had a staff to pay. When all the bills were met, Billy invariably made donations to local charitable institutions. Out of what was left he took approximately $100 a week for himself. The remainder, most often disconcertingly little, was used to make advance payments for the next crusade.

Ruth Graham was constantly perturbed about the family's financial state. After all, there was a growing family to support, a house to keep up and Billy's personal traveling expenses to be paid. All too often, Ruth had to telephone Billy and say: "You'd better send me a little money, dear. The bank is getting nasty again."

There were others who got nasty. In Atlanta, a newspaper reporter chanced, perhaps, to glance into the crusade office while the evening's receipts were being counted and subsequently wrote in his paper that Billy was making a fortune. Annoyed and embarrassed, Billy was forced to make a public statement of his accounts, showing where every penny went and how few of the pennies went to him. He learned his lesson. Thereafter he published a statement of accounts after each crusade.

When, therefore, the association was established, it was decided to settle the matter of Billy's income. In return for his services on the *Hour of Decision* and at the crusades, plus any writing he might do for the association, Billy was given a salary of $15,000 a year, which remained unchanged thereafter. In view of the fact that the association was soon operating on a budget of $2,000,000 a year, Billy's salary was a pittance that any businessman heading a corporation of similar size would have laughed at. But for Billy it was a phenomenal sum and he didn't know what to do with it all. Ruth, well trained in the meager economy of missionary life, continued to make her own clothes and most of what the children wore. She also liked to run her own home, without help or interference. Billy's new salary, then, more than twice his previous earnings, meant that they could pay off old bills and begin to save a little for the bigger home they wanted and needed for the large family they planned. The first thing Billy and Ruth agreed upon was that they would tithe; ten percent of Billy's salary was divided between the Baptist and Presbyterian churches to which they each belonged and at which they alternated their attendance when Billy was home.

Paralleling Billy's growth in popularity was a steadily increasing religious resurgence in America. Publishers became aware of the link between the two, and they hounded Billy for books. He wrote two: *Peace With God* and *The Secret of Happiness,* both of which were best sellers. Then a newspaper syndicate asked him to write a daily column, which was quickly purchased by almost a hundred papers. The writing meant additional income for Billy. But Billy saw no purpose in building up a big bank account. However, he was concerned about the future of his children, so he instructed his publishers and the syndicate to deposit their payments in a trust fund for the education of his children.

One day a Washington friend said to Billy: "Say, I hear you're having trouble with your income tax."

"Well, yes," said Billy. "Like everybody else, I have a little trouble paying it."

"Is that all that's wrong?"

"Yes. Why?"

"Oh, I just heard some talk."

The talk soon reached Billy. An agent of the Internal Revenue Department called on him. Billy produced his personal income tax records and said: "I'm sure you'll find everything in order. We've been very careful about keeping our records straight."

The agent glanced over the papers. "This is fine, as far as your salary goes," he said, "but what about your earnings from your writings?"

"Oh," Billy said easily, "I don't consider that income.

I don't even see the money. It goes right into a trust fund for my kids."

"Nevertheless," said the agent, "it's money you've earned, and you've got to pay a tax on it."

Once again Billy was embarrassed by his naivete about money, his lack of interest in it and his preference for putting his monetary affairs in other hands. Like thousands of other men, Billy Graham, the world's leading evangelist, had to scurry around to his bank and take out a loan to pay off Uncle Sam.

ii

In the five years following the important Los Angeles revival, Billy conducted crusades in 22 major cities—St. Louis, Dallas, Detroit, Houston, Minneapolis, Atlanta, Grand Rapids, Nashville, Toronto—back and forth across the continent. By now, a new concept in crusades had developed. Ordinarily, it was up to the individual evangelist to decide where he wanted to go, and when he got there he could only hope that his reputation and results would be enough to attract sufficiently large crowds to pay his bills and enable him to go on to the next stop. But there was no longer any question about Billy's ability to attract crowds and get results; the chore was to attract Billy. Demands on his time were great. It became necessary to plan crusades a year, even as much as two years, in advance. And there was no worry about paying bills. On the contrary, ministerial and lay groups in the requesting cities offered to pay for the crusade, including the expenses and salaries of Billy's team. Billy himself insisted that he receive nothing for such crusades. However, collections were to be taken up to support the *Hour of Decision* broadcasts, from which his annual salary was drawn. There were also to be allocations to underwrite a project that was high on Billy's hopeful list—crusades through Europe and the Far East, where, for many reasons, local funds were not available to cover the usual costs. In time, practically all of Billy's crusades were conducted in this manner, to the satisfaction of all.

Thus it was, early in 1954, that Billy and his team left for England upon the invitation and with the sponsorship of a thousand London ministers to conduct a rally in their city. As far as Billy was concerned, every crusade, held anywhere, was vitally important, but the London crusade was of special significance simply because of the immensity of the city. It provided Billy's biggest spiritual battlefield.

Added to this was the spiritual lethargy of the city. Less than ten percent of the people attended church with any regularity. The London clergy looked to Billy to provide the impetus that might fill the churches again, as they had not been in years. It was a great challenge, a wonderful opportunity, but a risk in view of the arrogant attitude of the London press. In the past, Billy had suffered the barbs of reporters at Birmingham who had called him the Hot Gospeler when he was there for a Youth For Christ rally. The London reporters were sharper. Even before his arrival they were calling the crusade a "Gospel Circus," and proclaiming that Billy's beliefs were 500 years behind the times.

Money was a factor in the London crusade. The local clergy could not possibly guarantee sufficient public support to cover the bills. Therefore the Billy Graham Evangelistic Association put up over $200,000, more than half the estimated expense, and to soften this blow at the association treasury Billy and his entire team volunteered to go on half-salary during the crusade.

The crusade was to be held in Harringay Arena, a huge structure with a 12,000-capacity. In years, the only person who had filled it was Winston Churchill. Now Billy was expected to fill it six nights a week for three months. Moreover, arrangements had been made to have the meetings broadcast on a closed-circuit to 400 smaller halls. The optimism of the London clergy overwhelmed Billy.

On the way to New York from Montreat, Billy stopped off at Washington. He had met President Dwight D. Eisenhower, visiting the White House previously at the President's invitation. Eisenhower urged Billy to call on

111

him whenever he was in the city. Billy had given Eisenhower a Bible which the President revealed he always kept on his night table. It was also at Eisenhower's suggestion that Billy had once preached on the Capitol steps.

Billy went to the White House on this trip. Although he made a rule of not disclosing his conversations with the President, he told reporters: "We discussed spiritual matters, then the President wished me luck in London and asked me to give the English people his greetings."

Later in the day, Billy encountered Senator Stuart Symington, of Missouri. The Senator said: "I hear you're going to London. So am I. We'll be there at the same time."

"Why don't you come around to the crusade?" Billy suggested.

"I'll be glad to," Symington said. "Senator Styles Bridges of New Hampshire will be with me. I'm sure he'll want to come, too."

"That's fine," Billy said. "I'll need all the moral support I can get."

"Friendly support," Symington said. "You've got all the moral support you need. Anyway, the English are fine people; they'll love you."

"I'm not worried about the people," Billy said. "Just the reporters."

The reporters did not even wait for him to land. When the ship was still well out of Southampton, a tugboat of newsmen came aboard and made directly for Billy.

Ruth was with him. Sensitive to the sedate English tastes, Billy had put aside the bright suits, loud ties and jazzy socks for which he had a preference and was dressed in a quiet grey checked suit and a simple tie. At his request, Ruth, who was usually a conservative dresser anyway, had dressed in black, but she thought Billy's idea that she not wear lip rouge was a bit too much and she refused.

The reporters fired a barrage of questions:

"Who asked you to come over here?"

"Do you think you're equipped to save England?"

"Haven't you got enough work to do saving America?"

"Is it true that you have no degree in theology?"

"Do you agree that most people need psychiatrists, not preachers?"

Billy answered all the questions simply, directly, with no attempt to be witty, no effort to acknowledge the cynicism.

One reporter asked Ruth: "Is it true that your husband carries around his own special jug of water for baptism?"

"Hardly," said Ruth. "My husband believes in total immersion, so it would have to be a mighty big jug."

On the hour's train ride to London, Billy, Ruth and Grady Wilson read the Bible and prayed. If ever anyone ever walked into a den of lions, they were about to. They prayed only for the gift of love, which they were so ready to give themselves.

Waterloo Station was packed. Billy, Ruth and Grady left the train apprehensively, but as they neared the crowd cheers went up.

"God bless you, Billy!"

"God love you!"

"See you at the crusade, Billy!"

"Britain needs you, Billy!"

Outside was even a greater crowd, carrying welcome banners, waving handkerchiefs and scarfs, singing hymns. Deeply moved, Billy made his way into the crowd, shaking hands, accepting enthusiastic slaps on the back, joining hymns, signing autographs. Two hours later, when the Grahams reached their hotel, they were exhausted from the fury but bouyant because of it.

Then they saw the latest papers and were quickly deflated. The reporters had been cruel. One paper, commenting on the crowd at Waterloo Station, headlined: "FILM STARS—SO WHY NOT BILLY?" Another bannered: "NO CLERICAL COLLAR, BUT MY! WHAT A LOVELY TIE!" In the Daily Herald, Socialist Hanon Swaffer wrote: "The man I most feel sorry for in this Billy Graham business is the Bishop of Barking, who, after an honored life, has become the American evangelist's best-known British sponsor." Cassandra, the columnist of the Daily Mirror, was outrageously snide, but with such clever control of the language that Billy was amused and immediately wrote that he would like to meet his critic. Cassandra replied in his column: "Will you meet someone fairly hell-bent and not averse to a little quiet wickedness? Why should we not meet in a pub called The Baptist's Head? You could drink what you choose while I sin quietly with a little beer."

Other factions also tried to make a fool of Billy. Among his pre-crusade appearances was a visit to the London School of Economics. The cynical students crammed the school hall. Introducing Billy, a professor said: "This is the first time a minister has been on our platform. We don't allow them here. This school was founded on secularism."

The remark brought a thunder of applause from the students. Beginning, Billy said: "I didn't realize that by coming here I'd be breaking your rules. But maybe the rules ought to be broken more often."

There was some amused laughter.

Then he said: "I know how you people feel, but I am going to tell you what Christ means to me and what He has done for me. You can take it or leave it."

He launched into a quiet and serious definition of his personal position. For several minutes, the students listened respectfully. Then one of them moved into the aisle. He assumed a crouched pose, jutted out his chin and lower lip, and began scratching himself like an ape. The students roared; Billy joined the laughter.

When the noise subsided, Billy said: "He reminds me of my ancestors." There was some laughter. Billy added: "Of course, all my ancestors came from Britain." Laughter exploded. There were no more interruptions.

But there was still no cause for confidence. The papers continued with their ridicule. At other public appearances there were more jeers and laughter. Placards announcing the crusade were ripped down. Although there were many encouraging letters, most of the mail was critical, antireligious, anti-American. No one dared anticipate how the crusade would go.

Then opening night came. It rained all day. Billy remained at his hotel, praying, preparing his opening sermon. A few telegrams of good wishes came, but they were from friends and were rather expected. They did not reflect the tone of the city.

At five, Billy bathed, shaved and dressed for the meeting. Just as he finished, the telephone rang. It was Jerry Beavan. "Things don't look so good, Bill," he said.

"What's wrong?"

"There's nobody here."

"It's early."

"Back home, we'd have a line a mile long by this time."

"Well, it's raining," Billy consoled.

"That shouldn't make any difference. It always rains in London."

"Nobody there at all?"

"A few. Maybe two or three hundred. That's a long way from 12,000."

"Things will pick up," Billy said, more to console himself than Beavan.

At six the telephone rang again. It was Senator Symington. "Billy," he said, "I've just left the Embassy. Ambassador Aldrich is of the opinion that it might not be a good idea for me and Senator Bridges to be at the crusade tonight."

Billy was crushed. "Oh? May I ask why, Senator?"

"Well, frankly, Billy," said Symington, "you appear to be a very controversial man in England."

"I guess so," Billy said. He tried to brighten his voice. "I understand, Senator."

"Anyway, Billy," Symington said, "Senator Bridges and I are due at a dinner tonight for Winston Churchill. It's been arranged for a long time; I didn't realize it would conflict with your opening. But I didn't want to use that as an excuse, Billy; I wanted you to know how things were."

"I appreciate that, Senator," Billy said. "Of course you oughtn't come. It might be embarrassing to the government if there's any disturbance."

"That's the point, Billy. I'm glad you understand."

115

"I do, Senator."

"Fine. Let's try to get together before I leave."

"I'd like that, Senator. Just let me know when you're free."

That was that.

Billy looked across the room at Ruth. "I'm scared to death, honey." He turned away and lowered his head. "Please, God, please, God, don't let me fail you."

At six-thirty, Billy and Ruth left their rooms and went downstairs to the lobby. The lobby was ominously quiet. Outside waited a car, put at Billy's disposal by the Ford Motor Company. He and Ruth entered it. The English chauffeur took his place in silence and began the eight-mile ride to the arena.

Billy was in agony. Sensing this, Ruth sat apart from him and did not speak. She knew there was nothing she could say, nothing she could do. It was all up to God. She looked blankly out the window and let her own prayers well up in her.

The rain had slowed home-bound traffic. The ride to the arena seemed interminable. Each time the car was stopped by a traffic jam, Billy sank lower in his seat and hid his head. At last the car pulled to the curb at the rear of the arena at the door where performers entered. There was no one in sight. The chauffeur got out and opened an umbrella as Billy and Ruth stepped from the car.

Suddenly the arena door opened and out ran a member of the London committee. "It's wonderful, Doctor Graham! It's glorious! There must be a million people in there!"

Billy stopped in his tracks. "We've got an audience?"

"The place is packed! And there are thousands on the other side of the building struggling to get in! We've had to put out a public-address system for them! I've never seen anything like it!"

Billy stepped back, his weary body leaning against the car. He looked up, letting the rain mix with his tears.

"Thank you, Lord, thank you with all my heart!"

The man grabbed his arm. "Come inside, come inside!"

As Billy went along, he asked: "Where did everybody come from?"

"I don't know. About 20 minutes ago they seemed to fall right out of the skies."

The noise backstage was ear-splitting as thousands of people loudly sang "All Hail the Power of Jesus' Name." So great was the sound that Billy could not hear the voices of workers who came up to shake his hand and wish him well. He was led into an office filled with dignitaries. Among them were Senators Symington and Bridges.

Symington made his way through the crowd to Billy and said: "I just had to come, Billy. While I was dressing, I couldn't get this meeting out of my mind, so I called Styles Bridges and said that, no matter what, we were going to be here tonight!"

"I'm so grateful," Billy said.

Other hands grabbed at him and began to lead him to the arena. As he ascended the platform the crowd saw him and acknowledged him by increasing the volume of their hymn. On the platform were bishops of the Anglican Church and other British religious leaders. In a special section near the front were members of Parliament and a battalion of respected leaders of all professions. Immediately in front were 300 newspapermen. As the hymn continued, Billy went among the men on the platform, shaking their hands and thanking them for coming. Then he took his place and joined the hymn.

At one point, the Bishop of Barking leaned over to him and, indicating the reporters with a discreet gesture, said: "Billy, I don't think you ought to give an alter call tonight."

Still too overwhelmed by the sea of emotion that surged at him from all sides, Billy was not fully aware of the intent of the suggestion, but he nodded and whispered: "All right." Through the rest of the proceedings, he was too dazed to think of anything except the gratitude that kept his heart pounding. When the time came for him to speak, he stepped forward and accepted the lapel microphone and Bible from Grady Wilson, then faced the crowd. He suddenly realized that his mind was a total blank. Later he revealed he had no idea what he had said.

In part he had said: "We have not come to save London. We are not here to try to reform you. We can only hope to light a little spark. We have come at the invitation of the leaders of your church to help them bring a spiritual awakening such as you have not had since Wesley."

On and on he went, the words flowing more from his heart than from the memory of the sermon he had prepared. He was too tense, too anxious for clarity of his purpose, to wander much through the space allotted him. He leaned against the sides of the pulpit and looked directly into the eyes of every person in front of him, surrounding him, above him. Before he realized it, he was speaking the words with which he usually led to the altar call.

"Now I want you to bow your heads," he said. "I want you to bow your heads and close your eyes. And I want you to pray with me. I want you to pray for the gift of faith. Ask Jesus to come into your hearts. He is here tonight, He is here in this arena, He is here, and you are here because He brought you here. Now this is your moment with Him, a private moment between you and Christ. He is listening to you; He wants to hear what you've got to tell Him. Tell Him you love Him; tell Jesus you love Him and want to serve Him and dedicate your life to Him. Tell Him that.

"Now I'm going to ask you something. You have said your prayer and Jesus has heard you. Now I'm going to ask you to show Him that you mean it, show Him and show yourself and show everybody in this great arena. Come forward, my friends, come forward and be a witness for Christ. People you know are down here, waiting to help you, ready to answer your questions, eager to send you into your new life for Christ. Come forward. Now let us all pray."

He bowed his head. The organ began to play softly.

that moment, Billy remembered the suggestion of the Bishop of Barking not to give the invitation. Well, it was too late. God had put the words into his mouth and he had said them.

He prayed. He heard a rustling, distant at first, then slowly nearing. He heard the excited murmurs in the press section. He prayed. He opened his eyes. In the half-moon of open space that separated him from the reporters a small crowd of men and women with bowed heads was gradually increasing. He could see more coming down the long aisles. He waited.

At last he said softly, so softly that only a few heard him: "My friends, you have just seen a beautiful thing —the love of Christ in action."

He left the platform.

iii

Despite the great crowd in the arena and the greater crowd outside and the greater crowd than that which listened to Billy by radio in 400 churches and halls across the country and despite the gratifying number of 222 inquirers who had come forward, there were still millions more in Britain who had been otherwise occupied that night, and what they would think of Billy Graham would depend greatly on what was written about him in the next day's papers.

The London *Times* reported:

"Far from being in bad taste, the service at Harringay last night was most demure. Surely there are already clergymen in Britain who are not only overswept by more passion but who command more of the demagogic parts than Mr. Graham."

The Manchester *Guardian* said:

"He has a holy simplicity."

The tide was beginning to turn.

There was still Cassandra. Billy met him, as he invited, in a pub, and while Cassandra drank his beer Billy sipped orange juice. They made a few jokes, then they got around to spiritual matters. The brilliant agnostic of London listened appraisingly to the unaffected farmboy from North Carolina. The next day, Cassandra wrote:

"He came into The Baptist's Head absolutely at home —a teetotaler and an abstainer able to make himself completely at ease in the spit and sawdust department a difficult thing to do.

"Billy Graham looks ill. He has lost 14 pounds in this nonstop merciless campaign. But this fact he can carry back to North Carolina with him. It is that in this country, battered and squeezed as no victorious nation has ever been before and disillusioned almost beyond belief he has been welcomed with an exuberance that almost makes us blush behind our precious Anglo-Saxon reserve

"I never thought that friendliness had such a sharp cutting edge. I never thought that simplicity could cudgel us sinners so damned hard. We live and learn."

iv

It was almost too much to be believed.

Every night for three months, despite the London rain and snow and fog, Harringay Arena was filled to capacity with overflows into the streets. One day Billy received a phone call at five in the afternoon: the arena was already packed and there were 35,000 people outside. Would Billy kindly hurry over and conduct a service so that at least some of the people could go home? That night Billy conducted three services. By the end of the crusade, almost two million people had listened to Billy in the arena, of which some 60,000 had responded to his invitation to come forward for Christ. There were thousands more conversions throughout the country, as the daily avalanche of mail vividly attested. Within the first weeks of the crusade, clergymen wrote Billy that people were filling their churches as they hadn't since the critical days of the war. The spiritual lethargy of England was rising dramatically.

Billy was as busy by day as he was at night. He

reached in Trafalgar Square. He went out to the factory districts to speak to the laborers. He toured the suburbs. At Cambridge University, dressed in his doctorate robes, he conducted a week of meetings that was carried by telephone to five other universities.

Ruth Graham was equally busy. Under her supervision were the 200 counselors especially trained to assist the inquirers every night. Long after the crowds had left, she was at the arena with her staff, sending follow-up letters to the converts, notifying pastors of churches near their homes, resolving the hundreds of problems that rose nightly. Reporters flocked to her for interviews, their early attitude of arrogance mellowing to submission. Teas were given for her, she visited hospitals and orphanages, and there were daily conferences regarding the crusade itself.

One day as she hurried through the city a young Englishman fell into step with her. "In a bit of a rush, aren't you?" he said. "Where are you going?"

"To my hotel," Ruth said.

"Time for a drink or a cup of coffee or anything?"

"No."

"Busy tonight?"

"I'll be at Harringay," Ruth said. "Why don't you come along?"

He dodged the question. "What about Tuesday night?"

"I'll be at Harringay then, too."

"Every night? Are you connected with Billy Graham in any way?"

"I'm his wife," Ruth said.

The young man bolted.

Other contacts with the British were of a far different nature. The House of Commons gave a luncheon for Billy, with prime-minister-to-be Harold Macmillan presiding. Sir Winston Churchill received Billy privately, then said: "I have been deeply impressed by him." Important titled Englishmen gave dinners and receptions. There were numerous cocktail parties at which, to the Grahams' surprise, the British clergy drank. The Grahams took orange juice, and after several such events Ruth commented: "I don't care if I never see another orange again."

There were some amusing faux pas. Unfamiliar with England's severe social distinctions and unable to distinguish his hosts from their help, Billy entered a formal dining room one day and beheld an elegantly dressed man, went to him and offered his hand, saying, "Your lordship, I don't believe we've met."

"I am your waiter, sir," said the man.

On another occasion, entering a private club, Billy was greeted by an important looking man who held out his hand. Billy took it and shook it and said: "Glad to meet you."

Frigidly the man replied: "Your hat, please, sir."

Queen Elizabeth II invited Billy to Windsor Castle to preach in the royal chapel to herself, Prince Philip and the Queen Mother. On arriving at the castle, Billy made a mental note about protocol. Inside the door, a man offered his hand. Billy held out his hat. The man took it. So far so good. Two young men came toward him and Ruth. From their clothes and their manner, Billy was sure they were part of the royal party. Actually they were two male secretaries who, sensitive to the social classifications even between employees in the castle, had not shaken hands with anyone above them or below them or even with each other since they had been hired.

Confident, Billy beamed his broad smile and grabbed at the hand of one, saying: "It's an honor. This is my wife, Ruth." And he turned to the second man. The two secretaries were appalled. The situation as saved when the Queen Mother entered the reception hall.

Now it was Ruth's turn. Knowing she was going to meet the royal family she had asked an English friend for instructions on the proper form of greeting. "A handshake and a curtsy," she was told. As the Queen Mother approached, Ruth frantically wondered if she should shake hands first then curtsy or vice versa or both at the same time. Dazzled by the beautiful woman, a woman of world importance, who came up to her, Ruth went through a quick, stiff, awkward maneuver that so startled

Billy that he reached out for her. She elbowed him away.

Later she said: "Why in the world did you grab at me the very minute I was curtsying to the Queen Mother?"

"I thought you'd tripped," Billy said.

It was soon evident that Harringay Arena would never hold the great hordes of people who wanted to hear Billy preach, and so it was decided to hold some of the services in the enormous stadiums of London. For one week, during which it poured rain every night, Billy conducted services at Wembly Stadium to crowds totalling 450,000. Among the week's 25,000 converts was Sir John Hunt, who had headed the expedition that climbed Mount Everest. Each night the Archbishop of Canterbury was present to give the invocation. On another occasion, Billy attracted a crowd of 185,000 to two stadiums. Nothing like it had ever happened before in the history of the country.

The last night of the crusade at Harringay was a holy bedlam. The arena was packed; the overflow stretched for blocks in all directions. Again the Archbishop of Canterbury was present, so was the Lord Mayor of London, so were more British dignitaries than had gathered in one place since the coronation. And in the press section was Cassandra.

If anywhere in London there was a firm evidence of what Billy Graham had achieved in the city, it was there in the press section. Undoubtedly the papers could have destroyed him, and certainly that was their intention his first days in the city. Whatever their motives, they had openly declared that Britain would not bow to this alien itinerant preacher who had come to London to show the British how to serve God. But Billy did not want to be bowed to; on the contrary, he was invariably the first to bow . . . to God. By his sermons, by his personal conduct in and out of the pulpit, by his humility and sincerity and warmth, by the ardor of his own faith, he entered the Harringay Arena a spiritual David and conquered the giants of the London press.

Surely there was other world news the day Billy Graham left London, but not much of it got into the newspapers. The *Evening News* put out a special Billy Graham Edition, proclaiming on its front page the words of Luke: "What went ye out into the wilderness for to see? A reed shaken with the wind? A prophet? Yea, I say unto you: much more than a prophet."

One reporter, more succinct and less dramatic, wrote simply this:

"Whatever it is that Billy Graham has got, he's got more of it than anybody else."

v

Long after Billy left London, pleas for a return to Great Britain followed him wherever he went. Thus a year later he was back, this time for a six-week All Scotland Crusade. Having heard the news from London, Scotland was ready. For that matter, Englishmen living in the north counties who had been unable to hear Billy in London went up to Glasgow. So great was the sustained interest in Billy throughout the entire land that the bomb-alert telephone system, set up during the war, had to be reactivated to bring the Glasgow services to eager listeners in 2500 municipal halls.

The only Glasgow paper to criticize Billy was the Communist *The Word*. Everyday it printed insulting limericks about Billy, any unflattering pictures it could find, and its biting report of each meeting made the audience look like pious fools. But *The Word* might well have remained unspoken. The Glasgow crusade was marked for success the minute Billy arrived in the city.

Crowds followed Billy and Ruth everywhere. Other papers printed every word Billy said wherever he chanced to say it. Kelvin Hall, with its 16,000 capacity, was filled every night and again loudspeakers had to be installed for those who lined the neighboring streets. On the first night, 470 men and women came forward in response to the call—more than at any other opening meeting in all of the crusades.

As in London, there were parties, receptions, dinners.

One day Billy found time to play golf, here in the land where the game was originated. As he approached one tee, his companions said: "Better skip this one, Billy. It's called Hell's Bunker."

Billy laughed. "Oh, no. I'll never give up to anything with a name like that."

Billy's return to Great Britain a year after the London crusade gave him the opportunity to ascertain the longevity of his effect. Some 40,000 people had been converted. To check on them all would have been impossible. Discussions with church leaders, however, disclosed that although a small percentage of the converts had fallen away the others who had held fast had brought friends into active religious life with the result that in most places attendance at church services and Bible classes was more than double what it had been when the London crusade ended. Thus the lasting effects of the crusade were unquestionable in the churches, in the homes, on the jobs and on the streets.

It was from Glasgow that Billy crossed over to the continent for the European crusades he had long wanted to conduct. For eight weeks he spoke through interpreters to Swedes, Danes, Norwegians, Germans, Swiss and French. He was in Geneva when a Big Four summit conference was being held and he called on President Eisenhower and Secretary of State John Foster Dulles. That day he told a rally: "The conference will not succeed unless Christ is made a member of it." It was a prophecy.

Significantly, the need of interpreters did not detract from Billy's personal impact upon his audiences. At each rally, Billy would speak two or three sentences, then pause for the translations. As serious an impediment as this might have been to his own concentration, it made no difference to the audiences. In fact, the interpreters were almost like background music: it was Billy the people heard, his personality and sincerity that came across to them.

In France there were some doubts about reactions to Billy in the predominantly Catholic country. And yet, like England, France was in a spiritual lethargy involving both Protestants and Catholics. Cautiously, Billy's friend in France estimated that at best he could expect on opening night in Paris some 5000 people, of whom perhaps a hundred might make decisions for Christ. The estimate proved too conservative. With little of the fanfare that had preceded Billy in London, Billy drew a crowd of 10,000 in Paris the first night, with over 600 conversions —another record. The figures held through the five-night crusade.

The Paris *Le Monde* said:

"Is not the availability of such crowds symptomatic in itself? It would be unjust for us to indulge in cynicism on the American style of such religious manifestations. Let us, then, acknowledge the spiritual dynamism of this man, whose formula and phrases may be infantile but who touches his listeners. His technique may offend European intellectuals, but nevertheless he is successful. The French Protestants who, with some reservations, invited Dr. Graham to our country did not make a mistake."

It was the same all over Europe. People did not come to listen with their minds, but rather with their hearts. And it was by reaching their hearts that Billy was able to bring them to Christ. Perhaps they knew this would happen to them; surely they hoped it would, and that was why they came to Billy in such great numbers.

The Geneva rally, organized at the last minute, filled a stadium and the surrounding hills. Thirty thousand people packed the Frankfort stadium. In Zurich it was necessary to use two stadiums, 200 yards apart, and 60,000 people came. At Mannheim, 1500 of the 50,000 audience made decisions for Christ; counselors were at their desks until dawn. That this should happen in areas where there was strong anti-American sentiments, where there was equally strong animosity between neighboring countries, and where religious fervor had lapsed shockingly since the war was, many said, miraculous.

Billy said: "It is the work of God. There is no other explanation."

Chapter IX

It was through the work of Ruth Graham that one of the family problems was solved. It was the problem of housing. There were now four children: Gigi, Anne, Ruth (called Bunny), and at last a son, William Franklin, named, Billy insisted, after his father, not himself. The little house in Montreat was getting crowded. When Billy was home there was no place for him to be alone to do his writing without having children barge into the room, and to have the private hours for his prayers and meditation he frequently had to get up at five in the morning. Moreover, the Graham house had virtually become a shrine for tourists. Each year the traffic increased. The endless parade of strangers who stared at the house, wandered across the lawn and approached the children was embarrassing and annoying. Something had to be done.

Through her personal thriftiness, Ruth had managed over the years to save enough to buy 200 acres of land on a mountaintop just outside Montreat. The property cost $12 an acre, a fact which clearly indicated its undesirability in the eyes of the average realtor. Ruth's dream was to build a home on the mountaintop someday, far away from the well-meaning tourists who unintentionally were complicating her jobs of running a house and raising her children.

But how to pay for the house? Regardless of his growing fame, Billy's salary remained at $15,000. Royalties from his books continued to mount in his publisher's office, but he refused to touch any of it. As soon as there was enough to guarantee the future of his children, Billy instructed his publishers that in his will he would specify the charities and missions to which he wished the rest to be given. His personal aversion to getting rich off his ministry thus remained unchanged.

Friends knew about Billy's attitude. They also knew that Ruth not only wanted but needed a bigger house and more privacy. Several of them therefore volunteered to provide the labor and the material to build the house, provided that they could remain anonymous in doing so in order that Billy could not seek them out and prevent them from demonstrating their affection and gratitude. Billy returned home from a crusade in 1955 to find Ruth bent over blueprints with an architect, and when he was told what was going on and that there was nothing he could do to stop it he sank back in his chair frustrated, a little angry, but deeply moved.

The responsibility for seeing the construction through to completion became Ruth's. When the floor plan was agreed upon, she told the contractors: "I want a new house that looks old."

"Just how do we build something like that?"

"I can show you easily. I've been dreaming about it long enough."

The house was built of logs hewn from trees that covered the mountaintop, which was practical because the trees were there, attractive because the natural colors of the property was retained, economical because the Grahams already owned the trees. Ruth wanted exposed chestnut beams and paneling throughout the first floor of the house. This could have been expensive, but on her drives around North Carolina Ruth had seen many old cabins that had been used as slave dwellings and were made of chestnut when it was more plentiful. To the astonishment of numerous farmers, Ruth started arriving at their doors with offers to buy the old cabins that stood, most often empty and unused, in far corners of their property. Because of the cost of dismantling the cabins and hauling the usable lumber to the mountaintop, Ruth limited her price to $50 each, which in some cases required some hard bargaining on her part. Several of the cabins had floors of brick that had become smooth and polished by the years; the bricks ended up as the downstairs flooring of the new house.

In the same way, Ruth furnished most of the house. Avoiding expensive antique stores, she went from farm to farm, buying old but excellent pieces that fitted well into the chalet-ranchhouse type of home she wanted. She made her own draperies, from material that cost a quarter a yard. Because of the beautiful view of the Smokies, she had broad picture-windows installed in every room, saving the best view for Billy's study.

He told her: "I can't work with all that scenery staring at me." He turned his desk around and put his back to the window. She let him have his way.

On another occasion, Ruth got her way. She disliked washing dishes, and with four growing children in the house there were always so many of them. Repeatedly she hinted to Billy that she could well use a dishwasher, but he seemed not to hear her. That autumn she was ill for a week and Billy had to do the dishes. That Christmas he gave her a special gift: the machine.

Another happy feature about the new house was its inaccessibility. In helping design the house, Ruth gave calculated attention to the road leading to it. It was a dirt road, narrow, steep and winding, with inclines of almost 70 percent in some places and hairpin turns that only a skilled driver or a desperate man would attempt. Here, thankfully, no tourist-buses could come. To discourage autos, Ruth saw to it that no identifying signs were erected. On the contrary, signs were put up that announced: PRIVATE ROAD, DANGEROUS ROAD, NO TRESPASSING and NO CARS BEYOND THIS POINT. There was another sign: BEWARE OF VISCIOUS DOG. Billy was so amused by the misspelling that he refused to have the sign corrected.

There was indeed a dog, but he was not vicious. He was Balthasar, a big white Pyrenees, almost the weight of Billy and equally as gentle. He was a one-man dog and Billy was the man. When Billy was away, the dog knew he was not permitted in the house and did not try to enter, but the minute Billy drove up to the door and rushed inside to greet his family, Balthasar was at his heels, confident that he would not be put out. Billy loved animals, which was undoubtedly a hangover from his youth on a farm. In addition to Balthasar, there were at least two others dogs around the house, several cats, birds, a mule and, for a time, a ram. The ram departed quickly one morning after butting Billy from behind and causing him to limp for several days. Often the animals were gifts; equally as often Ruth was forced to be firm in refusing them in order to keep the mountaintop from becoming a zoo. For that matter, Billy was always receiving gifts, usually things his devotees had made themselves, gifts ranging from jams and jellies to paintings and cufflinks. At the opposite extreme, he was once given a white convertible which, because of his boyhood love of cars, overjoyed him. Then he realized how inconsistent it was for a man who repeatedly denounced worldly attachments to possess such a gaudy car, so he gave it to his secretary.

Occasionally people asked Ruth how badly she minded being without Billy so much of the time. There were years when he was away four weeks out of five. She replied: "Of course I mind it. I miss him. But I feel that by keeping up his home, raising the children and providing a peaceful, loving place for him to come when he is free I am sharing in his ministry."

Unquestionably, Ruth faced unusual difficulties. She was determined that Billy should be head of the household and she raised the children in that atmosphere. Even when he was away for long periods, all major decisions were left to him. He wrote or telephoned everyday; either in writing or on the telephone Ruth put household problems to him, whether they pertained to the house itself or a special request of one of the children. She made a habit of referring to Billy repeatedly during the day, she read his letters to the children and they shared the telephone calls. Thus the children grew up knowing that although their father was frequently away his influence was always with them.

Becoming a wife, mother and housekeeper did not

diminish Ruth's interest in religion. She had her private meditation and prayers before the children awoke; as the children matured she taught them to adopt the same daily practices. This did not prevent them from burdening Ruth with normal children's pranks and problems. They turned out to be as rowdy as all children, perhaps more so with 200 acres to romp in. Actually the religious atmosphere of the house provided unique puzzles in child-raising. One day Ruth heard screams from infant Bunny and rushed into her room to find Anne slapping the baby.

Ruth rushed forward. "What in the world are you doing?" she demanded.

Anne said: "I'm teaching Bunny her Bible."

"What do you mean?" Ruth asked, annoyed.

"I'm teaching her to turn the other cheek."

In other ways, the Bible was a more calming influence. A Bible student herself, Ruth was seldom without the book. As she went about the house at her chores, she carried the Bible with her from room to room. As she sewed, she would pause to re-read a portion she wanted to understand better. She would stop in the middle of making a bed to read a few favorite verses. In the kitchen as she waited for a cooking meal to reach the serving moment she would hunt up the Bible answer to a special problem someone had presented to her. When Billy was home their conversation was often of a religious nature. As familiar as he was with the Bible, he would nevertheless ask her for pertinent verses to support a point he wanted to make in a sermon. Sometimes Ruth would mention a passage she was having difficulty grasping and they would talk it out. And when an event occurred in her day that fulfilled a particular Bible message she would go to him eagerly and tell him about it.

A friend who knew of Ruth's early desire to be a missionary once asked her: "Do you ever feel deprived or disappointed or out of things because you're running a home instead of a mission station?"

"I believe," Ruth answered, "I am a home-maker by divine appointment. I prayed a long time over the decision I had to make, and I believe now that God wanted me to marry, that He wanted me to marry Billy and take care of his home and his children. Being a wife and a mother is a vocation, too, you know."

With this attitude, it was therefore appropriate that Ruth should install over her kitchen sink a sign that read: "Divine services conducted here three times daily."

And yet religion did not introduce an air of solemnity into the house. That would be scarcely possible in a house of four growing children—five children, when Edman Nelson was born in 1958. Nor would it be possible in a house where the husband and wife shared so deep and open a love, shared also the excitement of knowing their lives were wholly dedicated to the work of God. Always there were recent triumphs for God to stir their gratitude, always there were plans for future triumphs to stir their hopes, always there were new worlds.

ii

In 1956, Billy set out to speak for Christ in the far corners of the world. The major country on the tour, at least in terms of the time he would spend there, was India. Out of India's 400 million population, there were only ten million Christians, evenly divided as Catholics and Protestants. The country was poor, there was widespread disease and illiteracy, and its leader, Prime Minister Jawaharlal Nehru, was an openly admitted agnostic. In addition to this, just a few weeks before Billy's arrival in India, the country had been extensively toured by Nikita Khrushchev, the world's Number One Communist. Plainly, Billy did not stand much chance for success in India.

On reaching India, Billy paid a courtesy call on Nehru and he was in the Prime Minister's office just a few minutes when he began to feel the personal visit had been a mistake. Nehru was cool. He indicated clearly that he was busy; he had traveled through India with Khrushchev and now work had piled up on his desk; he did not have time for courtesy. Their first moments together, Nehru impatiently fingered a letter opener.

Billy said: "President Eisenhower has asked me to convey to you and your country his warmest regards and affection."

"Thank you," said Nehru. "And mine to him."

"Mr. Dulles also asked to be remembered," Billy went on, "and he especially wanted me to asssure you and your people of the friendship of all Americans."

"We return the friendship," Nehru said, his eyes on the letter opener.

Billy said: "I'm looking forward to this visit to your country. I've read so much about India; it has a beautiful culture and holds an important place in the world."

"I hope you enjoy your visit," said Nehru, and he glanced at the clock on the wall.

"Thank you, sir," Billy said. "We're all hoping, sir, that you will be able to attend one of our meetings."

"I will try, but—" Nehru shrugged his shoulders and indicated the work on his desk.

Billy realized he was getting nowhere. He moved to the edge of his seat. "Mr. Nehru, I'm not the man for all this diplomatic talk. I know I'm intruding upon you, but I wanted to be able to meet and tell you precisely why I'm here. I am a preacher, Mr. Nehru. I believe in Christ, I believe He can change people's lives, I know He has changed mine. I want to give that message to your people. Now I know that few of your people are Christians, that most of them think Christianity is a Western religion. That just ain't so, Mr. Nehru. Christ belongs to India and India belongs to Christ, and the more Indians I can convince of that the happier I will be. I promise you, sir, that I don't intend to force my religion on your people, but I'm going to tell them about my religion, about what I think it can do for them and their souls, and they can make their own decisions."

Nehru put down the letter opener. "I admire your directness, Doctor Graham," he said. "Christianity is not new here, as you know. It is believed that one of the Apostles reached India, and the work of St. Francis Xavier some 500 years ago made a lasting impression.

If there are not more Christians in India it is not because the people have been unreceptive. Of course, I have read books about Jesus Christ; I find Him a fascinating personality. I wonder, do you have time to answer a few questions for me?"

The two men settled back in their chairs. Outside the door, Nehru's staff, bearing problems from all over the world, sweated and fretted for more than an hour.

The Indian crusade was another record-breaker for Billy, not only as far as his own records were concerned but the records of the Russians in India as well. In Madras, where Khrushchev had attracted a crowd of 22,000, Billy drew 40,000. It was the same all over the country. In Delhi, where there were only 10,000 Christians, 20,000 people came to the rally. Evidently he was reaching Hindus and Moslems as well as Christians, and because of this he sometimes changed his sermon topic at the last minute so that he could impart some basic knowledge about Christ as well as define His influence on the individual life.

Billy was impressed by the behavior of the Indian audience. No matter how big the crowd, the people were always well behaved, quiet and respectful, not only toward him but toward each other. Their natural reserve was often surprising. Numerous times Billy awoke early for his meditation and would step outside for the early sun and find hundreds of people waiting silently there for him to lead them in morning devotions, many of them waiting three or four hours. So quiet, so orderly, had they been that if he had not stepped outside he would not have known they were there.

He noticed, however, a tendency of the people to want to get close to him, to touch him, and he began to realize that many were regarding him personally with the same reverence they showed their Hindu holy men—as something sacred, special and apart from other men. Billy discussed his suspicions with some missionaries and when they conceded that this was probably happening he was terrified. "Not I, but Christ," he insisted in subsequent talks. "If you are here because of me you are wasting your time, but if you are here because of Christ then you will profit through all eternity."

Thereafter he was sternly cautious against any personal adulation; he would not even answer questions about himself put by reporters unless they pertained to his own conversion and his faith. "Unless I am speaking about Christ," he said, "I have nothing important to say."

Thousands came to hear him speak about Christ. In three days at Kottayam, he addressed 125,000 people. Many of them came from great distances. One man had walked four days to cover the hundred miles to Billy; it was common to hear that some in the crowds had traveled 500 miles to attend a rally. The final rally attracted over 200,000. On the platform with Billy were Indian Christian leaders, missionaries, delegates of the diplomatic corps, princes and rajahs. Present also was the man Billy least expected to see: Jawaharlal Nehru.

From India, Billy continued eastward, conducting one-day rallies in Bangkok, Manila, Hong Kong, Formosa, Seoul, Tokyo and Honolulu. For the most part he traveled in non-Christian areas, but invariably the press said of him: "Billy Graham is here to bring God and men closer together, and in this great work he deserves all praise and support." A Japanese paper stated: "Dr. Graham speaks universal truths. They go beyond national boundaries, racial differences, even religion divisions. The common denominators of faith, humanity and peace are with all men who believe in the Divine Being, whatever their personal approach." And a Honolulu paper bannered across its front page: "YOU HAVE A DATE AT 3 P. M. TODAY—KEEP IT!" The date was, Billy quickly clarified, with Christ.

The trip took eight weeks. During it Billy had spoken to millions of people; thousands of them publicly made their declarations for Christ. These conversions were vital because, in Billy's opinion, they were evidence of Christ's readiness to fill a human heart the moment it was opened to Him. But Billy was aware that surely there were many private conversions at the rallies and that there were others of such delayed action that weeks or months might pass before a man discovered in himself the quietly growing convictions that would lead him to Christ. How often this happened, Billy could not possibly know, but always in his prayers was the plea that those who left the rallies unconvinced would nevertheless brood on the words they had heard and that perhaps someday the irresistible truths would overwhelm their doubts and overpower their hearts.

It was thus with joy and exultation that, on a Sunday in April, 1961, five years after he had been in India, Billy Graham announced on the *Hour of Decision:*

"I have just learned that one of the famous agnostics of the world, a man of great power and influence, has put aside his doubts. In India, Prime Minister Jawaharlal Nehru has publicly disclosed that he now believes in Almighty God. Praise be to the Lord!"

iii

In his appeals to his audiences for the acceptance of Christ, Billy often said the acceptance would "take you from victory to victory to victory." Billy himself was following that same route. From city to city, from country to country, he went from victory to victory. Beginning in 1954, he had his sights on the biggest victory of all, the potential victory that held the greatest challenge:

New York City.

That was the year a group of important New York laymen approached Billy Graham and asked him to conduct a crusade in their city—the largest city in the world, the most vital and the most vitalized of cities, the city which stood more in need of a spiritual resurgence than any other in the country. Of the city's millions, only 43 percent claimed any church affiliation, only 7½ percent were active Protestants. Even in pagan countries there were cities that could boast a better Christian-action rating than New York.

The sheer size of the city required the utmost preparation for a campaign. Billy had been in New York many times, he had appeared on New York television and radio and been interviewed by New York papers, he had addressed special groups. But a crusade was something different. The word itself indicated a broadside attack. To make itself felt in New York, the crusade would have to be a combination of the avalanche of the Rocky Mountains and a trans-Atlantic tidal wave. More organization would have to go into it than a Presidential campaign, more teamwork than winning a World Series, more money than exchanged hands on the New York Stock Market on a good day.

Nevertheless, when the lay group asked Billy if he would conduct a crusade in their city, he answered simply: "With God's help, yes."

For two years, Billy kept New York uppermost in his mind. Wherever he was, whatever was going on, he met with his staff regularly to discuss the New York crusade and to pray for its success. Every aspect of it was discussed, then discussed again, and if, after one feature of it was settled, anybody came up with a new and better idea, the entire crusade plan was re-evaluated, reshaped. At last Billy felt his team was ready for some positive action.

In the spring of 1956, Jerry Beavan went to New York to meet with the group that had suggested the crusade, a group now expanded to include some of the city's leading clergymen. Beavan rented an office just off Times Square, then met with the group. It was headed by George Champion, president of the Chase Manhattan Bank, and some of its members were William Randolph Hearst Jr., Henry Luce, Captain Eddie Rickenbacker, Dr. Norman Vincent Peale, Dr. Dan Poling and Ogden Reid.

Beavan told the rich, important, influential men that it was Billy's plan to conduct the rally at Madison Square Garden, capacity: 19,000. Yankee Stadium and the Forest Hills Tennis Stadium would be necessary for one-shot outdoor rallies. The crusade would run from May 15 to September 1, 1957, the longest crusade in Billy's career. Estimated cost: $2,500,000. Staggered by the price tag,

137

the group decided to go ahead nevertheless. New York needed Billy.

Familiar problems appeared. Of New York's 3,000 ministers, about half were unconvinced that the crusade would do any good. According to annual custom, the circus would occupy Madison Square Garden for a month in the spring, this time right before the crusade. Some ministers ventured the opinion that the fundamentalist-type of crusade they felt Billy conducted might give the impression that the circus had been held over. The task of changing their minds fell to Beavan and Grady Wilson. Between other crusades, Grady hurried to New York to call on New York ministers, man by man, and to speak to ministerial groups in the suburbs. Whenever hold-outs seemed too adamant, Billy himself went into the fray. Slowly, over the course of months, the opposition diminished.

Then came the job of organizing the Greater New York area to establish prayer groups, collect a choir, train counselors and schedule attendance at the rally by communities so that everyone would have an equal opportunity to attend. Moreover, travel agencies began to advertise the crusade as a summer feature of a New York vacation. So many people signed up for such tours that an entirely new factor in the attendance had to be taken into account.

Six months before the crusade was to begin, 10,000 prayer groups were organized, placed under the supervision of Mrs. Norman Vincent Peale. Grady and Jerry Beavan had spoken in hundreds of churches in the New York area to alert congregations for the rally. Billy had addressed fund-raising breakfasts and dinners, at which almost $2 million were pledged. From around the world had come 200,000 letters and cards, promising prayers and donations.

By March, 1957, any New Yorker who didn't know that Billy Graham was coming to town had to be in a coma. All over town, 650 billboards heralded Billy's arrival; 40,000 phone-dial cards were distributed, bearing the words: *Pray for Billy Graham*; 40,000 bumper stickers and 40,000 windshield stickers appeared everywhere, and 35,000 stores displayed window placards. A month before the opening date, Grady went on radio and television twice a day to discuss the crusade and past crusades. On all such appearances, Grady announced a telephone number which people could call any time of the day or night to talk over their personal problems with a crew of ministers.

During these preliminary weeks Billy was at Montreat, spending most of his time in meditation. He had his sermons ready, but he knew that often when he got up to speak his prepared talk vanished from his mind and he let whatever words come out that God chose to give him. Therefore he felt he needed God now more than ever. Smart, sophisticated, cynical New York would demand more than the old words served up on new platters: it would demand the full influence of the Spirit.

The house on the North Carolina mountaintop was quiet. The children were sent to their grandparents in Montreat, every precaution was taken to keep out visitors, to silence the telephone, to cut off telegrams and mail. With only Ruth present, Billy underwent a spiritual retreat for the strength to face the great city.

He once said to Ruth: "I have prayed, worried and wept over New York more than any other place in which we have held a crusade. Sometimes I have stood in the middle of that city and wondered if I could ever reach it for God."

Their last morning at Montreat, Billy and Ruth went for a walk around their property and played for a while with their four sheep—the latest addition to the Graham menagerie. Then they prayed together and discussed Scripture. Then they packed and left.

To be sure, every crusade held its own challenge, and its success, the spiritual throb it stimulated, was Billy's only evidence that God was continuing to use him. Nothing else mattered. If attendance was poor, if there were few conversions, if he was obviously failing to reach the people, then Billy would know his ministry was over: God had chosen another man for the job. Billy's anxiety, then, was always that what he did was pleasing to God, and it was only by the results of the crusades that he would know. Everything must be for God.

On arriving in New York a few days before the rally he was appalled to see his picture in every shop window and on every lamp post. He commented:

"One of the things that has sickened me has been the concentration of publicity around my name. As quickly as possible this gaze on me and our team must be shifted to the Person of Christ. I must decrease and He must increase. I have expressed often that God will not share His glory with another. When any one man becomes the center of attention, he is in danger of eclipsing his ministry. Thank God for all interest that has been stirred among people everywhere, but it is my prayer that the interest will be focused in Christ."

But the interest in Billy Graham mounted when the news got out that he was in New York. There were press conferences, interviews with leading columnists, appearances on television shows, dinners, receptions, street rallies throughout the area. Billy had arrived in New York rested and in excellent health; within a week he was showing the strain, and he had three brutal months to go.

The night before the crusade, a run-through was held at the Garden. There were still many rough edges, and it was well after midnight before Billy was able to return to his hotel. Exhausted, he let himself fall on the bed. His outstretched arm touched the Bible on his nighttable. Picking it up, he flipped through its familiar pages. Then his eyes fell on the twenty-fourth chapter of Ezekiel...

". . . .Woe to the bloody city. I also will make the pile great. Heap on the logs, kindle the fire, boil well the flesh, empty out the broth and let the bones be burned up. Then set it empty upon the coals, that it may become hot and its copper may burn, that its filthiness may be melted in it, its scum consumed. I the Lord have spoken it: it shall come to pass and I will do it. . . ."

It was a message for New York, a warning. Billy knew now what it was he must tell the people.

The next day when a reporter asked him what his goal was for New York, Billy said: "To save the city from itself by sending the Christians back to their churches."

The churches were evidently as eager for the return as Billy was. Much of the success of the rally was attributable to their efforts. The first night, delegations came from 112 different churches, and every night of the three-month crusade churches were responsible for about 7,500 of the capacity attendance. To some observers, this looked as though the attendance was rigged: Billy didn't have to worry about an empty auditorium as long as the churches were bringing in their congregations by the busloads. To Billy, the reverse was the case. The backbone of Christianity, he frequently said, was with those who at least made the effort to fulfill their obligations. The heart, however, was with those in churches who had given their own hearts utterly to Christ. A man could attend church all his life without being a complete Christian, but as long as he was attending church there was a chance for him. Was it not possible that the very salvation of New York, of the world, for that matter, was with those who needed only a nudge to elevate them from religious habit to religious fervor? Then let the church-goers attend the crusade. Let them be the advance guard in the conquest of the world for Christ.

So the New York crusade began, that May 15, 1957, and day after day until September 1st, it was a tornado of superlatives. Each night the Garden was packed, producing at the end a live audience of 1,687,000. The Saturday night rallies were televised, reaching an audience of millions more. In the Garden, 56,000 people made decisions for Christ. From the mail it was learned that another 60,000 made the same decisions as a result of the telecasts. At street rallies throughout the city Billy tied up traffic for hours. He drew a bigger crowd into Times Square than New Year's Eve, bigger than V-J Day. He packed 100,000 into Yankee Stadium, with 35,000

turned away. Crusade-trains came from as far away
Memphis, Toronto, Akron and Omaha. Celebrities came
Jane Pickens, Ed Sullivan, Vice President Richard M
Nixon, Sonja Henie, Gene Tierney, Alvin Dark, Ca
Erskine, Greer Garson, Perle Mesta, Adolph Zuko
Pearl Bailey, Ethel Waters, Jack Dempsey, Dale Evan
Equally important in the eyes of God were the uncel
brated, the ordinary people, who came night after nig
to listen, to pray, to decide.

It could not be said that New York was easier fo
Billy than London or any other place. True, his receptio
was warmer: of all the New York papers, only the Co
munist publication criticized him, but that was to be e
pected. But Billy worked harder in New York than els
where, never resting, taking little time for sleep or foo
preaching in rain or shine or New York's sweltering he
at every opportunity, hearing out a worried man in a
elevator or the man who cut his hair or the man wh
tugged at his sleeve at a busy corner. Let it be said, the
that New York was Billy's greatest success because, mo
than anywhere else, the city realized its need for Bi
and what he had to say and thus was ready for him whe
he arrived.

Billy put it another way. In the closing ceremony
the Garden, he said:

"In our spirit of dedication and in our spirit of humili
and dependence upon the spirit of God, we may not s
you again until we meet at Jesus's feet. What a ti
that is going to be. It won't be long for some of us. We
all be there.

"What a hope we Christians have! Down here v
have suffering, misunderstandings, many times persec
tion. But up there! Up there, the Bible teaches, t
Church, in the coming of Christ, shall gloriously triump
And if you are in Christ, you are on the winning side.

"Here, in this year of 1957, God has done a great wor
"To God be the glory!"

Chapter X

When Billy got home from New York Ruth had only one worry about him: his lost weight. In all other ways, he was in perfect shape. The success of the New York crusade had sent his spirits high, his morale soaring. He was like a fighter who, having won the championship, was physically exhausted but emotionally ready for another 15 rounds. It was up to Ruth to calm Billy down and restore his strength so that when the next battle came he would have the stamina for it.

From her years in China Ruth had acquired a preference for Oriental food and a skill for cooking it. But Chinese cooking never completely satisfied Billy. He enjoyed the taste but even when he over-ate he still felt a little hungry. Ruth therefore had to learn to cook Southern-style—chicken, mashed potatoes, greens, all in big portions.

Returning home after a crusade, Billy usually put all work aside for a few days and took advantage of the Nature wonders around his home. His favorite relaxation was long walks deep into the hills where he would not encounter people who might want to talk to him. When invited to do so by his friends, he would go hunting for bird or deer as long as they kept on the move. He lacked the patience to wait for the birds or deer to come near him. He also lacked patience for still-water fishing; sitting unoccupied in a boat for hours unnerved him. Swift-river fishing was a different matter: at least there was always the task of trying to stay on his feet. He liked golf because of the action in it, and he played the game swiftly, moderately well, and sometimes with too much chatter for his companions.

Actually Billy's health was unusually good. On crusade he occasionally caught colds because of the relentless pace he maintained and his determination to keep outdoor preaching dates whether it was raining or snowing. In Germany he developed a kidney stone which put him in a hospital. Coincidentally the East Germany Communists, seeking to smear Billy's reputation, chose that very night to report that he had been seen entering a hotel room with a voluptuous blonde. "They were wrong," Billy later said. "The only blonde hair I saw that night was my own as I pulled it out of my head in pain."

Rather than submit to surgery at the time and thus disrupt the crusade, Billy postponed his operation until he was able to return to North Carolina. Several people wrote and asked if they could have the stone for a souvenir, which both amused and annoyed Billy.

Another operation he underwent in North Carolina was the correction of a right inguinal hernia. His father-in-law, Dr. Bell, performed the operation. As was usual in abdominal surgery, Dr. Bell decided to have a look at Billy's appendix while he had him open and found it acutely inflamed; he removed it. Dr. Bell also treated Billy the time the ram butted him, causing some torn ligaments in his leg.

In 1959, overwork caused a spasm of a blood vessel in Billy's left eye, causing his vision to blur. The damage was serious, but not as serious as some reports indicated. Nevertheless, hundreds of people around the world wrote Billy and offered to have their eyes transplanted to his by surgery. The offers blurred Billy's vision even further —with tears. However, doctors felt that rest would repair the injury, and after a few weeks away from books, mail and the glaring lights of arenas Billy was cured and restless to get back to work.

Otherwise Billy's illnesses were mild. To provide energy while on the road, Dr. Bell prepared a medicine for Billy containing minerals and vitamins. In New York Billy was stricken after a meal and took a dose of what he thought was the medicine. Next morning he was so fully recovered that he bragged to his staff about the wonderful medicine in his bathroom cabinet. One man went to look and came back with the only bottle he could find. "Is this the stuff?" he asked.

"That's it," said Billy. "Great stuff. If you're ever sick take some."

The man pointed to the label. "It's hair tonic," he said, "clearly marked for external use only."

Billy winced, then remarked: "Well, I guess from now on I'll have to have real close shaves."

Billy's ability to laugh at himself provided the equilibrium to keep him from becoming concerned about himself. At times his close friends wondered how he could take all the blatant adulation without following the course of other celebrities who, in the same position, became temperamental, hypochondriac, hostile and self-centered. The most obvious answer was his own faith: trusting so much in God he did not fret much about himself. Another answer was his appealing, self-deprecating sense of humor.

At one press conference a reporter asked Billy what his I. Q. was. Billy said: "Not very high, I guess, but I don't know. I've always been afraid to have it determined."

At a London press conference he sent instructions ahead that he would discuss only evangelism. A reporter threw out the question: "What do you think of Senator McCarthy?"

Billy answered: "I didn't know he was an evangelist."

Billy's staff often went to great lengths to put his sense of humor to the test. Once he bought a new hat of which he was especially proud. Grady Wilson filled it with shaving cream, then called in several people as Billy prepared to put it on to go out. When the cream oozed down Billy's face and neck, the people roared with laughter—and Billy joined them. But he got even with Grady. On a boat trip to Europe, Billy got hold of Grady's seasickness capsules, emptied out their powder and filled them with hot mustard. Each time Grady complained: "I don't know what's wrong with these pills, they work but they give me awful indigestion," Billy doubled with laughter and kept his secret until the boat docked.

One night Billy's mother happened to be standing near him as he got ready to enter an arena to preach and she noticed that his shirt collar was open. She said: "Billy, I forbid you to go out in front of all those people with your collar open."

"If you forbid me," said Billy, "then I'm telling you I won't preach tonight."

"Why not?"

"Because," Billy said, "with my collar buttoned my Adam's apple can't joggle up and down and unless it does I can't talk."

Morrow Graham attended the closing sessions of the London crusade and she was also at New York. On both occasions, Billy introduced his mother to the great audiences. Both times she was given an ovation. In London a woman turned to her and said: "I've wanted to thank you for years for giving the world a son like Billy."

Morrow Graham answered: "For years I've been thanking God for giving him to me."

In Atlanta, while his mother was in the audience, Billy said: "If I am a Christian today it is because I was raised in a Christian home." To Morrow Graham, this was her finest tribute.

Innumerable times Billy showed the same public respect and devotion to his wife. Before the New York crusade, Dorothy Kilgallen, the Hearst columnist, went to Montreat to interview Billy, and she later reported that Ruth had the occasion to enter Billy's study seven times during her visit: each time Billy stood up to greet her. "A real Southern gentleman," Miss Kilgallen observed. More accurately, a real Christian husband.

In his sermons on Christian family life, Billy never hesitated to use Ruth as an example, describing her own spiritual life, her methods of instilling Christian ideals into the children and her manner of settling problems of child-raising in a Christian way. One night, sitting next to her mother, young Gigi Graham whispered: "Why can't he keep all that to himself?" But for Ruth the invasion of privacy was the highest flattery. It meant Billy was content with her, their children and their home, that her prayers for fulfillment as a wife, mother and housekeeper had been answered.

ii

Surely one factor in Billy's vivid appreciation of his home and his family was that his ministry kept him away from both so frequently, thus enhancing his joyful hours at Montreat and sensitizing him to the spiritual riches he always found awaiting him when he returned home. After New York, demands for crusades increased in such proportions that Billy was on the road almost continually. Grady jokingly observed that it might be a good idea for him and Billy to take up a sideline of Fuller brushes again because of the tremendous areas they were scheduled to cover. Wherever they went they met the same glowing reception, and when they left they left behind the same glowing spirituality.

The highpoint of 1958 was the San Francisco crusade, conducted for packed crowds from April 27 to June 22. Once again Billy's team of 36 skilled workers faced enormous problems. As in New York, there were more church delegations requesting reserved seats than could be accommodated without depriving others. Every night, 18,000 people jammed the Cow Palace, and there were times when the crowd outside was so great that Billy had to go out to address them. Again there were thousands of conversions, again a great city of the world was transformed. For Billy, there was a moment of special sentiment in San Francisco. On the platform with him opening night was Mordecai Ham, the evangelist who had called Billy to Christ 23 years earlier at Charlotte.

The following year Billy undertook what was certainly the broadest crusade of his career—the entire continent of Australia, plus New Zealand and the surrounding islands. In seven weeks he criss-crossed vast Australia, making air hops the distance equivalent between New York and Rome. In Sydney alone 980,000 attended the rallies, with 56,780 conversions. One afternoon it was necessary for him to address a crowd of 150,000 in tw adjacent stadiums. Before the crusade was over, Bill faced more than three million people, a fourth of Australia's population. To provide the proper follow-u with those who made decisions for Christ required volunteer staff of 40,000 counselors and advisors. Bill admitted: "I am dizzy with the thought of what is happer ing here."

It was also in 1959 that Billy went to Moscow. Th visa he was granted did not permit him to preach, bu when the news circulated that he would attend service one Sunday at Moscow's Baptist church over 2,500 peo ple turned out just to look at him and watch him pray fo them. He asked to be taken to the mammoth Lenin Sta dium and in the center of its field he knelt and praye that one day its 100,000 capacity would be filled wit people who yearned to hear the Gospel.

On his preaching tour of the Caribbean earlier, Bill had gone into South America for one-day rallies. Thus in 1960, when Billy went to Africa, he became the onl evangelist in history to preach on every continent. On seven-week tour that took him to 16 cities in nin countries on the African continent, he preached Christ' message beneath a broiling sun to crowds greater tha any that had gathered before. Because of the many dif ferent tribal languages in some countries, he often had t use five or six translators to relay his words to th crowds but this obstacle did not dim the impact of wha he had to say. The people understood him. When the moment of decision came, they went forward. In Liberia the daughter of President Tubman was one of th first to proclaim her decision for Christ in response t Billy's invitation.

Billy said much to touch the African heart. Often h pointed out: "Jesus loves Africa, and I will tell you why When the angel warned Joseph and Mary that Kin Herod would be looking for Jesus to kill Him, it was neces sary for them to flee to safety. They could have chose any place in the world to go, but where did they go? The came to Africa. Africa gave protection to Jesus when He needed it. That's why Jesus will always protect Africa."

In a land seething with nationalism and extremely sensitive to racial matters, Billy daringly voiced his own convictions on brotherhood when he said: "Let me tell you something. Christ's skin was only a little lighter than yours and a little darker than mine. So any way you want to look at it, Christ is the link between us that makes us one mankind, judged by Him by the way we treat each other."

There, neatly and succinctly, was the summation of the purpose that sent Billy Graham to every corner of the world. He believed that all mankind was one brotherhood, created by God to love Him and serve Him in this world and to be happy with Him in the next. It was a message for all nations, all races, for people of all ages. To the elderly in their twilight years it gave the promise of even more happiness than raising their Christian families had brought them. To the middle-aged it provided a spiritual anchor on the tempestuous seas of a world torn by strife, anxiety and uncertainty. To the young it was a bold signpost at the crossroads that would determine their futures.

Billy never lost his concern for youth. His early years with the Youth For Christ movement had taught him how eagerly the young sought spiritual guidance, how quick they were to accept it, how lost they knew they were without it. Billy therefore responded speedily at Easter, 1961, when he was called by the mayor of Fort Lauderdale, Florida, to speak to the thousands of college students who had flocked to the resort city for what had become an annual Easter vacation of what the students called the Four S's—surf, sun, suds and sex.

Billy was already in Florida, completing a three-month crusade in the state. He knew from newspapers what was going on at Fort Lauderdale, and when the appeal came from the mayor he re-arranged his schedule so that he could go there. Nobody knew what to expect. The city was a shambles of carousing students, empty beer cans, wrecked cars and battered private property. There was every possibility that any students who came to hear Billy would come to ridicule him. And there was the equal possibility that none would come at all.

A stand was installed on the beach, with loud speakers pointing in all directions. When Billy arrived to talk he found that a crowd of 10,000 awaited him, and from their tone he could tell they were there for fun. Dressed in a dark suit, well-tanned, and looking as handsome as any student in front of him, Billy seemed as though he was still in college himself, and at first he sounded like it.

"I don't see what all the rumpus is about," he said. "You don't look like such a bad crowd to me. It's vacation time, you've been working hard all year, you deserve a little fun. I'm beginning to wonder if the grown-ups around here haven't been exaggerating things."

There were cheers, whistles and a roar of clapping hands.

Billy said: "I didn't mean for you to applaud that hard."

Smiles now, chuckles, some laughter. The students were warming to Billy. He understood them.

"I was thinking today about myself at your age," Billy went on. "I remember roaring through the streets of Charlotte in my car, ringing a cow-bell, my girl friend at my side, both of us having a lot of innocent fun—until the policemen drove up. There were other things like that, too, but I'm not going to tell you about them."

More approving chuckles and laughter.

Billy's voice grew tense; he raised his tone. "But there's something I want to ask you. What do you believe in? What is your philosophy?"

A student called out: "Sex!"

Billy hesitated. He could not ignore the boy, he dared not retreat. He said: "A fellow down here said sex. Sex is a fine and beautiful thing. None of us would be here without it. But none of us deserve to be anywhere if we abuse it."

Then he lit into the students, talking to them bluntly, directly, sometimes sharply. There were no more interruptions.

Of all the places in the world where Billy had spoken, there was probably no place least suitable for an altar call, but Billy realized he must offer one, he must let this crowd see that even here on the beach of Fort Lauderdale where they had caroused for a week, Christ was waiting to enter their hearts. So when he finished talking to them, Billy asked the students to join him in prayer. Across the wide beach, thousands of heads bowed, and from the loud speakers came Billy's voice, asking Christ to go among the young people surrounding him and to stir in them the spiritual stamina by which they could come forward and publicly make their decisions for Him.

A few students began to move forward, then more and more, until at last, gathered around Billy were over a hundred of them.

It was fitting that this scene should occur, in Florida among the young, for it was just 20 years since Billy himself, at the age of the converts now surrounding him, had in another corner of Florida pledged his life to Christ to the extent that no girl, no friend, nothing at all, would ever detour him from the service of God to which he dedicated his entire self. In the years since that day Billy had gone all over the world to win souls for Christ. Who knew but that one of the young people now with him might be inspired to follow in his footsteps? The world could well be waiting for precisely that decision.

At the moment, the world was waiting for Billy. As he had done once before, he would go out from Florida to everywhere. In May, he would be back in England, this time for a crusade at Manchester. In July there would be a crusade in Minneapolis; in August he would be in Philadelphia. The years would be full: in 1962, Billy would make two trips to South America; and there would be a rally in Los Angeles in the spring, a crusade in Chicago in May, another in Germany in August, another in Boston in November, then back to India, and after that in 1963 would come Dallas and Tokyo and Buffalo and New Zealand and. . . .

Was there a man of God alive who more vividly

obeyed Christ's command: "Go ye forth and teach all nations!"

And wherever he would go, in quest of one soul or a million of them, Billy would arrive with the words that had become his most uttered prayer, the prayer that had become his trademark at the end of his *Hour of Decision* broadcasts, heard by millions every week around the world:

"May the good Lord bless you—real good!"

PAPERBACK LIBRARY TRINITY BOOKS
By Frances Parkinson Keyes

ST. ANNE, GRANDMOTHER OF OUR SAVIOUR

"written with fervor, with reverence and with warmth. . . . The book has charm, beauty and inspiration."
—Boston Sunday Herald

"The only complete presentation in English of one of the most beloved Saints in the Church."
—Forecast: Catholic Literary Supplement

"A godsend for any devotee of St. Anne."
—The Ave Maria / Catholic Home Weekly

53-396, 60¢

BERNADETTE OF LOURDES: SHEPHERDESS, SISTER AND SAINT

". . . will delight all who read it." —Newark News

"One of the most delightful, inspiring books in years . . . the story is so intimate, so unusual that we can recommend it to persons of all faiths." —El Paso Herald Post

"An engrossing and human picture of the saint and her times."
—Bridgeport Post

53-414, 60¢

THREE WAYS OF LOVE

The inspiring stories of St. Agnes of Rome, St. Frances of Rome and St. Catherine of Siena—three memorable women whose lives centered on a love for God and humanity, and who achieved immortality through that love.

"Accurate, authentic, absorbing." —Virginia Kirkus

53-429, 60¢

THE ROSE AND THE LILY

"Frances Parkinson Keyes works anew her memorable magic in bringing us fascinating studies of St. Rose and St. Marian."
—Catholic Digest

"Colorful and authentic." —Chicago Tribune

"Inspiring." —Catholic Forecast
53-460, 60¢

If you are unable to obtain these books from your local dealer, they may be ordered directly from the publisher.

PAPERBACK LIBRARY, INC.
Department B
260 Park Avenue South
New York, N.Y. 10010

Please send me the following books:
I am enclosing payment plus 10¢ per copy to cover postage and handling.

Book 53-396 St. Anne, Grandmother of Our Saviour..No. of copies....

Book 53-414 Bernadette of Lourdes...............No. of copies....

Book 53-429 Three Ways of Love.................No. of copies....

Book 53-460 The Rose and The Lily..............No. of copies....

Name ....

Address ....

City .... State .... Zip Code ....